The Counsel of Many

The Counsel of Many

SELECTING YOUR PERSONAL ADVISORS

Gary A. Sallquist

Dimensions for Living
Nashville

THE COUNSEL OF MANY:
SELECTING YOUR PERSONAL ADVISORS

Copyright © 1999 by Dimensions for Living

This book is printed on acid-free paper.

Library of Congress Cataloging-in-Publication Data

Sallquist, Gary A., 1938-
    The counsel of many : selecting your personal advisors / Gary A. Sallquist.
        p. cm.
    Includes bibliographical references.
    ISBN 0-687-07700-1 (pbk. : alk. paper)
    1. Christian men—Conduct of life. 2. Christian men—Religious life.
3. Consultants—Miscellanea. I. Title.
BV4528.2.S25 1999
248.8'42—dc21   98-46650
                                                                            CIP

Scripture quotations, unless otherwise indicated, are from the Holy Bible: New International Version. Copyright © 1973, 1978, 1984 by the International Bible Society. Used by permission of Zondervan Bible Publishers.

Scripture quotations noted NRSV are from the New Revised Standard Version Bible, copyright © 1989, by the Division of Christian Education of the National Council of the Churches of Christ in the United States of America.

Scripture quotations noted NASB are from the New American Standard Bible, © The Lockman Foundation 1960, 1962, 1968, 1971, 1972, 1973, 1975, 1977.

99 00 01 02 03 04 05 06 07 08 — 10 9 8 7 6 5 4 3 2 1

MANUFACTURED IN THE UNITED STATES OF AMERICA

CONTENTS

ACKNOWLEDGMENTS

My energy for writing this book has come from the constant nudging of the Holy Spirit and the unfailing support and encouragement of my family. Thanks to them, I hope the book will be a worthy contribution to God's Kingdom.

Thanks, first and foremost, to Joyce—the most important person in my life. You have been with me through a challenging and rewarding business career, through the rigors of seminary, through my first pastorate, through my work at Promise Keepers, and now PhilanthroCorp. You have clearly qualified for sainthood! Thank you for joining me on this wild and wonderful ride, our Christian spiritual journey.

Thank you, Susie and J. P., our daughter and son-in-law. I appreciate your encouragement, your notes, your love, and your genuine friendship. Thank you, Steve and Chrysa, our son and daughter-in-law. I love and appreciate you. It's been said that children are a message we send to a time we will not know. Mom and I are proud to send both of you "kids" forward as our message!

Emma and Liam, our grandchildren, you are a joy to behold, and we can hardly wait to see what God does in and through you!

Thank you to my brothers in Pi Kappa Alpha, who were "family" before I really had a family. Thanks especially to Brad, Ralph, "Foots," Dusty, and all the rest of you.

I am grateful for the love and friendship of my brothers and sisters in Christ at Princeton Theological Seminary, College Hill Presbyterian Church, Evangelical Community

Church, Boulder Valley Vineyard, Promise Keepers, and my accountability groups.

I owe many thanks to the people with whom I have developed and utilized the concept of the personal advisory team, especially Tom Wilkinson, Ned Patrick, Pat Patrick, Bob Patrick, Mike Moore, Joe Barker III, Bob Marriott, Mike Kessling, Jim Zazanis, Earl Ray, Jack Pomeroy, and Steve Crone.

A special thank you to Peter Goodwin for his highly competent help in shaping the manuscript for this book—and for his efficiency in helping both of us hit the necessary deadlines. He became a friend and respected colleague in the process.

This book is especially dedicated to my mentor, lifelong friend, and fraternity brother, the Reverend Simon A. Simon. Si went home to be with the Lord in March 1998. His spirit undoubtedly gladdens heaven, just as it lives on in the lives of his family and friends!

I love, respect, and appreciate all of you and thank you most sincerely for the way God uses you in my life!

INTRODUCTION

Plans fail for lack of counsel, but with many advisers they succeed.

(Proverbs 15:22)

In the book of Proverbs, wisdom is the most highly praised of all God's gifts. Proverbs instructs,

> Make your ear attentive to wisdom,
> . . . .
> If you seek her as silver,
> And search for her as for hidden treasures;
> Then you will discern the fear of the LORD,
> And discover the knowledge of God.
> (Prov. 2:2*a*, 4-5 NASB)

According to God's Word, wisdom is a gift from God, graciously bestowed, but bestowed only on those who truly long for it and seek it. We gain wisdom not simply by following our instincts or by trial and error. Rather, we learn from God's Word and from wise teachers.

God has placed many teachers in each of our lives. If we will take the time to seek out these teachers and cultivate relationships with them, our lives will be enriched beyond measure. I know this is true, because I have seen it happen again and again in my own life and in the lives of others.

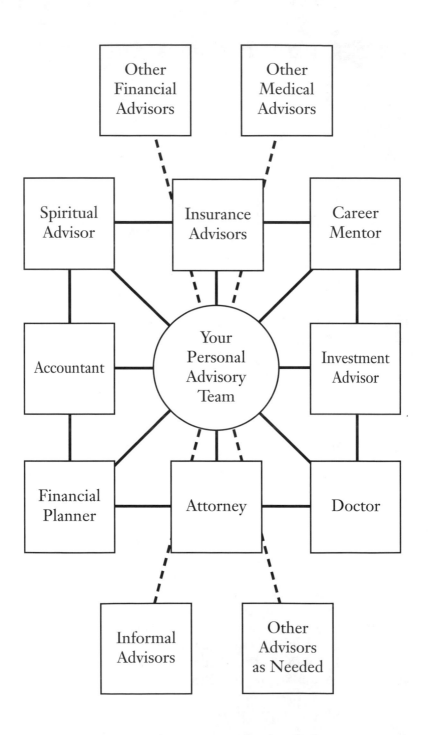

The Personal Advisory Team: A Personal History

My professional career began in the management training program at a major corporation, where I received little personal attention or individualized instruction. After a few years there, I changed careers and joined a life insurance firm owned by a man who would become a lifelong mentor and friend. I spent seventeen years in this firm, learning the business firsthand from a man who took a genuine interest in my professional and personal development. My experience working at this firm taught me the value of having a personal career mentor and spurred me to think more about the blessings and benefits of forming meaningful personal relationships in the business world.

Within this firm, I operated my own business. I left my position there in order to do a merger with a company in Cincinnati; and then I relocated from Omaha to Cincinnati in 1981. My firm offered various types of insurance coverage for business and estate-planning purposes. As the business grew and we began offering some investment and consulting services, our clients began asking us to advise them regarding other aspects of their finances.

Our clients' requests gave birth to the idea of the personal advisory team. My partner at the time, Tom Wilkinson, and I quickly realized that we were not knowledgeable enough to advise our clients in all their financial affairs; but we also recognized a need for a coordinated planning process that would utilize the expertise of professionals in various fields. Tom and I worked with a network of financial professionals, and we were happy to refer our clients to the professionals who could help them make the best financial decisions. We realized that we were doing much more than making referrals: We were coordinating and serving on personal advisory teams.

When we began directing these referrals and communicating with the other professionals who were advising our clients, the results were truly remarkable. Our clients gained a better understanding of their finances and thus were able to make more well-informed decisions regarding investments, insurance, long- and short-range planning, saving, and spending. The various aspects of their finances began to work in concert. Most satisfying to our clients was that they were better able to articulate and achieve their goals for their money.

As our clients gained more understanding of and control over their finances, many of them began to be more interested in making their money count for something. My career experienced a natural progression into the world of charitable giving. Our firm designed, implemented, and coordinated major gifts between donors and charitable organizations. In this work, I learned how much good can be done for the Kingdom of God through proper financial planning and charitable gift planning.

When I was called to leave my business career and enter seminary, I thought I would put away my business skills; but time has proved me wrong. In my studies at Princeton Theological Seminary, in my work as pastor of adult education at College Hill Presbyterian Church in Cincinnati, and in my work in planned giving for Promise Keepers men's ministry, and now for PhilanthroCorp, I have returned time and time again to the concept of the personal advisory team.

It's Not Just for Finances Anymore

When Tom and I first began thinking of the personal advisory team, we thought of it primarily, if not exclusively, as a financial tool. In fact, the seed for the concept was planted in my head by Napoleon Hill's secular classic, *Think and Grow Rich*, a book that focuses exclusively on the attainment of monetary wealth. I read this book several times before I became a Christian, fascinated by the "Master Mind" con cept Hill introduces, defined this way: "Co-ordination of effort of two or more people who work toward a definite purpose in a spirit of harmony."[1]

After I accepted Christ as my personal savior, I reevaluated some of my financial goals, and I thought about Hill's book in a new light. I appreciated his emphasis on teamwork and cooperation. He adapted the "Master Mind" concept from Andrew Carnegie, a man who adroitly utilized the cooperation of many people: "Mr. Carnegie's Master-Mind group consisted of a staff of approximately fifty men, with whom he surrounded himself for the definite purpose of manufacturing and marketing steel. He attributed his entire fortune to the power he accumulated through this Master Mind."[2] However, I knew that neither Carnegie nor Hill had fully understood the way God works in the midst of believers when they are working together: "Again, truly I tell you, if two of you agree on earth about anything you ask, it will be done for you by my Father in heaven. For where two or three are gathered in my name, I am there among them" (Matt. 18:19-20 NRSV).

God can do awesome things through believers who work together, believing God's promises and seeking God's will. But God doesn't provide us with financial resources simply for our own pleasure. God intends for us to use what He provides wisely and in a way that honors Him.

As I have applied the concept of the personal advisory team in my own life and seen it applied in the lives of others, the concept has broadened to encompass every aspect of a person's life. The advisory team has functioned as a channel for God's spiritual, relational, and material blessings.

One of the greatest blessings I have received by having my own personal advisory team has been *integration* of the many facets of my life. We are often inclined to divide up our activities and responsibilities into categories: spiritual and secular, career and home, work and play. Financial planning, legal planning, and the like may seem to be interruptions in our home life and irrelevant to our spiritual life. But I have learned that when I have the guidance of a living, breathing person in these seemingly technical areas, the borders between spiritual and secular, career and home, work and play become less distinct. My values have always been reflected in my financial decisions, but I haven't always been so deliberate or successful in making financial decisions that honor God and advance the work of the Kingdom.

The personal advisory team helps us see that God cares about the technical aspects of our lives—our medical needs, our legal matters, our financial dealings, and our careers— just as much as God cares about our family responsibilities, our inner thoughts and dreams, and our spiritual growth.

Building Your Own Personal Advisory Team

Anyone can benefit from a personal advisory team, but in this book I am going to focus specifically on professional, Christian men who desire to integrate their spiritual goals and values into every aspect of their lives.

You probably already have some form of a personal advisory team in place. You probably have a personal physician and insurance agents, and you may have an attorney, an investment broker, an accountant, or other advisors whose professional advice you value and trust. But unless you have deliberately cultivated your relationships with these professionals and have attempted to work with them to formulate an integrated life plan, you are not reaping the full benefits of an advisory team.

If you decide to form your own advisory team, there are two basic factors that you should consider when looking for any personal advisor: *professional competence* and *personal compatibility*.

Professional Competence

Most of the advisors on your team will serve you primarily in a professional capacity (your career mentor and your spiritual advisor being the primary exceptions). You will pay them for their services, and you should approach the relationship in a professional manner. Certainly, you will be taking your professional relationship with these advisors to a deeper, more personal level than is often the case, but you should not forget that you are hiring them because they have the professional capacity to perform particular tasks.

There is no reason to "let your fingers do the walking" in the process of choosing an advisor. Calling doctors, attorneys, insurance agents, and other professionals simply because you see their advertisements in the Yellow Pages is not the best way to find the right advisor for you. Instead, seek referrals from friends and colleagues, and research and study the potential advisors' professional credentials.

As soon as possible, you should meet with the potential advisor in his or her office. Even if the advisor is a personal acquaintance or friend, be professional in your dealings with this advisor. You may set up an initial interview or meeting to discuss your needs and decide if the potential advisor can help you meet those needs. You may even wish to meet the advisor's staff and colleagues.

Although you know your own goals and needs better than any other person does, you are probably not equipped to make the best decisions in many technical matters without the advice of an expert. Many of your advisors will have spent many years in graduate study and continuing education in order to learn their professions. No matter how well you know your own body, unless you have devoted many years to the study of medicine you probably don't know the best way to address your health problems. No matter how methodically you keep your own financial records, unless you continually track them you probably aren't aware of all the changes in tax laws that have gone into effect this year. This is why you need a doctor and an accountant. When you seek an advisor, you should settle for nothing less than an expert.

Personal Compatibility

Because, as I have mentioned, you will be taking your relationship with your advisors to a deeper level than is often the case, it is important to find advisors who share or at least understand your values, goals, and needs. Professional competence is extremely important in an advisor, but it must be accompanied by personal compatibility.

Although you may build enduring friendships with some of your advisors, this is not a requirement, as long as you can connect on more than a strictly professional level. Nor is it necessary that all your advisors be your same age or your same sex. However, the best advisors are usually fairly close to your age and share a fair amount of common ground with you. On some level, most of your advisors will be peers.

There are some cases in which age and sex are particularly important considerations. Because you will be sharing very intimate, personal matters with your spiritual advisor, it is best for your spiritual advisor to be your same sex. As a Christian man, you will probably be able to be more open and honest about every aspect of your spiritual, religious, and moral life with another man than you would with a woman. For similar reasons, I also recommend that your career mentor be a man.

Because you will come to them for their wisdom and experience, your spiritual advisor and your career mentor should be considerably older than you. Your other advisors should be closer to your age. It is not prudent for a thirty-year-old businessman to be advised by a sixty-year-old man in legal, medical, or financial matters. When the young man grows older himself (and his finances are more sophisticated, his medical needs more abundant, and his legal needs more complex), his attorney, doctor, and financial advisors will be retired or deceased when he most needs their help. In these areas, it is best if we can mature together with our advisors.

Differences in age, sex, and interests aside, the most important factor to consider when evaluating personal compatibility is whether your advisor genuinely cares about you. Does he or she treat you as a valued customer? just a paycheck? Or does he or she seem genuinely concerned about your well-being? Does he or she communicate with you openly and encourage you to do the same? Your advisor needs to understand your needs in order to help you meet them, and there can be no understanding without open communication.

A final aspect of personal compatibility is *spiritual compatibility*. As I have worked with Christian men in helping them create their own personal advisory teams, I have often been asked whether every advisor on the team must be a Christian.

The Scriptures offer some guidance on this issue. In 2 Corinthians, Paul writes, "Do not be bound together with unbelievers; for what partnership have righteousness and lawlessness, or what fellowship has light with darkness?" (6:14 NASB). Many Christians believe that this verse suggests that we should not conduct business with, receive instruction from, or even associate with people who are not Christians; but I believe this is a misinterpretation. Paul uses the words "bound together" to indicate a very close alliance. I believe this verse instructs us not to enter into alliances such as business partnerships and marriages with unbelievers. However, I do not believe that the advisor relationship is the same kind of alliance.

Clearly, your spiritual advisor must be a Christian, and if at all possible, your career mentor should also be a Christian. Furthermore, none of your advisors should be antagonistic toward Christianity or unsympathetic to your Christian beliefs and values. The more closely your advisor's values are aligned with your own, the better the chemistry between you will be, the more open your communication will be, and the higher the trust level between you will be. However, the best professional advisors will not always be Christians.

Remember that you work with most of your advisors on a professional level. Your primary consideration in choosing advisors such as your financial planner, your insurance agents, and your doctor should be their professional competence. If you are not able to find an expert advisor in a certain area who is also a Christian, do not rule out the possibility of working with an advisor who is not a Christian. Instead, prayerfully seek the Lord's guidance in finding the advisor who will best serve your professional needs.

Whether or not a particular advisor is a Christian, I recommend discussing with him or her some of the areas in which your Christian values will most directly affect your work with the advisor. For instance, you may talk with a potential accountant about your practice of tithing; you may discuss with your investment advisor your wish to avoid certain stocks that do not align with your Christian values; or you may discuss with a potential financial planner your desire to make financial gifts to your church or other Christian organizations. Find out how your advisor feels about these issues, and make sure that he or she can help you be a good steward of your resources.

In Romans, Paul writes, "Do not conform any longer to the pattern of this world, but be transformed by the renewing of your mind. Then you will be able to test and approve what God's will is—his good, pleasing and perfect will" (12:2). As Christians, we are called to live our lives in the world but to constantly *renew our minds* through prayer and study of the Scriptures. We are called, not to withdraw into cocoons or enclaves of Christianity, but to take our beliefs with us into the world.

If one of your advisors is not a believer, you will certainly have opportunities to witness to him or her. Your financial and legal planning and your care for your own body should reflect your Christian values, and the way you live your life as you interact with your advisor will be the greatest witness of all. In the words of St. Francis of Assisi, "Preach the gospel always; if necessary, use words."

The Members of Your Advisory Team

Every man's needs are different, and consequently no two personal advisory teams are exactly the same. You may need a primary advisor in an area where I will rarely need advice or assistance, and vice versa. Nevertheless, there are certain key advisors who will serve on almost every Christian man's personal advisory team: a spiritual advisor, a career mentor, a financial planner, insurance advisors, an accountant, an investment advisor, an attorney, and a doctor.

You will certainly rely on some of these primary advisors more than others, but you will probably need the services of each of them at some point in your life. In addition to these primary advisors, your advisory team may include a number of other advisors, depending on your needs: medical specialists, financial professionals, and others.

If you are a young man, just beginning a career and perhaps without many financial resources, beginning to build a personal advisory team now will help you more than you can imagine. As you grow older, more established in your career, and more mature in your relationship with the Lord, you will develop an integrated approach to your career, your finances, your health, your spiritual life, and your long-term goals. If you are an older man, perhaps established in your career and mature in your relationship with the Lord, your advisory team will help you refine your planning and maintain a physically, spiritually, and financially healthy lifestyle throughout your later years.

Wherever you are in your life's journey, your career, and your Christian walk, the members of your advisory team can help you put your faith into action in every aspect of your life.

NOTES

1. Napoleon Hill, *Think and Grow Rich* (North Hollywood: Wilshire Book Company, 1966), 190.
2. Ibid., 193.

C h a p t e r   O n e

YOUR SPIRITUAL ADVISOR

The teaching of the wise is a fountain of life.
(Proverbs 13:14)

Every member of your advisory team will share special knowledge that will help you follow God's will for your life, but none will be so integral to your spiritual life as your spiritual advisor.

Your attorney may well be a wise and godly person, but you go to an attorney for *knowledge* of legal matters—not for spiritual *wisdom.* Your doctor may have a rich relationship with the Lord, but you seek a doctor for medical *expertise*, not spiritual *wisdom.* To be sure, you should welcome wise counsel wherever you find it, and as you begin building a personal advisory team, you are sure to find it in many places; but you should also make a deliberate effort to find one person upon whom you can rely as your spiritual advisor.

Finding a Spiritual Advisor

Many men, even though they may love the Lord and desire a meaningful relationship with Him, never experience true joy and fulfillment in their Christian walk, primarily for one reason: they don't know how.

Having a relationship with Jesus Christ does not require any special knowledge. God gives us that gift by grace if we are willing to accept it. But understanding the depths of God's grace; discerning the wisdom of God's Word; and developing a meaningful, productive spiritual life do not come automatically. Experiencing the fullness of God's grace requires discipline, practice, study, and openness to teaching.

Frequently, the process of spiritual advising happens naturally, without much intentional planning. But more often, finding a person who will guide you in your Christian walk requires a deliberate effort on your part. If you do not already have a person with whom you meet regularly in order to receive spiritual instruction and guidance, you can take three initial steps to find one: (1) Identify people whose spiritual life you admire; (2) Pray for God's direction; and (3) Ask the person you have identified to consider being your spiritual advisor.

1. Identify the people whose spiritual lives you admire. If you will think about the Christians you know, surely you will think of a few who exemplify the abundant life in Christ. Perhaps you recognize in them certain traits or habits that you would like to incorporate into your own life, or perhaps you admire their grasp of Scripture, or perhaps you simply sense a certain quality about them—a pure heart, a generous spirit, a loving soul—that appeals to you. You know these people for a reason: God wants to use them in your life! One such person could probably become your spiritual advisor.

The process of spiritual advising requires a serious commitment from both the advisee and the advisor. As you seek a spiritual advisor, look for a person who can commit to meeting with you regularly (perhaps an hour every week or every two weeks). Your spiritual advisor should also pray for you consistently and be available in times of spiritual crisis.

As I mentioned in the introduction, because you will be sharing very intimate, personal matters with your spiritual advisor, it is best for your spiritual advisor to be your same sex. As a Christian man, you will probably be able to be more open and honest about every aspect of your spiritual, religious, and moral life with another man than you would with a woman.

Most often, this advisor will be an ordained minister or a leader in your church. Your spiritual advisor does not have to be the senior pastor of your church—he may be an associate minister, a deacon, a Sunday school teacher, or a group leader—but he should be actively involved in the life of a Christian congregation.

2. Pray for God's direction. Initiating a relationship with a person who will influence your personal relationship with God is a significant step in your Christian walk. Your choice of a spiritual advisor should be guided by prayer. Ask God to lead you to the right person—the person God intends to use in your life for this purpose.

3. Ask the person you have identified to consider being your spiritual advisor. Some churches formally establish spiritual advisor relationships, coordinating laypeople with "spiritual directors"; but in most churches, you will have to initiate the process. From my own experience as pastor of a church, I know that a pastor is *never* short of things to do. Associate ministers, deacons, and other church leaders all have many responsibilities both inside and outside the church, as well.

However, this is no reason to hesitate to ask someone to consider being your spiritual advisor. A person who is called to Christian service is called to be involved directly in people's lives. If God intends a person to be your spiritual advisor, and if that person is open to God's direction, that person will make time for you.

If you set this process in motion, the relationship will be

good for both you and your advisor. Your initiative will show
your potential spiritual advisor that you are serious about
your spiritual growth.

The Process of Spiritual Advising

Consistency, trust, and prayerfulness are foundational to
any spiritual advising relationship. *Consistency* maximizes the
value of your time with your spiritual advisor. You may meet
weekly, biweekly, or monthly—whatever the two of you
agree upon. Of course, if either of you has a last-minute
emergency, you can reschedule. Being too tired to rise early
for a breakfast meeting, however, does not constitute an
emergency! Make your time with your spiritual advisor a
high priority.

Without *trust*, your relationship with your spiritual advisor will remain superficial and stagnant. Be open and honest
with your spiritual advisor, and expect the same from him. If
you are to have a meaningful relationship with your spiritual advisor, you must communicate openly—especially
about the things that may be difficult for you to discuss.
Make a covenant that you will each "tell it like it is." Agree
that your conversations together are confidential and that
whatever you discuss will remain between the two of you.

An attitude of *prayerfulness* will nurture the trust between
the two of you. Just as you prayed for God's direction in finding the right spiritual advisor, you should continually pray
that God will be in the midst of your relationship with your
advisor. Bathe the process in prayer: open and close your
time together with prayer, and pray for each other in
between your meetings.

Once you have established a foundation of consistency,
trust, and prayerfulness, you and your spiritual advisor will
need to decide how to structure your meetings. If your spiritual advisor has served others as a personal spiritual advisor,

he will bring his own experiences of what works well, but keep in mind that no two relationships are exactly alike. Your strengths and weaknesses, your successes and challenges are uniquely yours, and you probably have many good ideas about how to address them.

I suggest beginning the process by defining a spiritual path that you want to follow. You can set specific mileposts along the path and even plan a timeline for reaching those mileposts. For example, if you are struggling to spend time reading and reflecting on God's Word every day, you may set specific goals such as, "Next week, I will not go more than one day without reading my Bible and reflecting on what I read for at least five minutes; the following week, I will figure out the best time of day for me to read and reflect on God's Word, and I will set aside half an hour each day for that purpose; by a month from now, I will have made spending time in God's Word a regular part of my daily routine."

A spiritual advisor of mine helped me reach my goal of reading my Bible every day with a simple suggestion. He encouraged me to leave the morning paper in the drive-way—not even bring it in the house—until I had finished my quiet time with the Lord. If I ran out of time in the morning, he pointed out, it would be far better to give the sports section the short shrift than to neglect my time in God's Word. We prayed together that I would have the discipline to follow his suggestion and meet my goal. When I put this suggestion into practice, I saw results. It was exciting to me to see measurable progress toward my spiritual goals.

Most men like to see immediate results. That is part of how God "wired" us. Sometimes we look at spiritual matters as if they are general, vague, or nonmeasurable; and this perception can keep us from devoting our best energy to our spiritual life. When we get over this fallacy by setting specific mileposts and working toward them, our spiritual lives begin to flourish.

Your spiritual advisor can help you articulate your goals for your spiritual life and help you meet those goals by praying for you and offering practical, concrete suggestions. But perhaps the most important way your spiritual advisor can help you meet your goals is by holding you accountable.

Accountability and the Spiritual Advisor

Accountability is an essential element of spiritual growth. Once you have set a spiritual path for yourself, with specific mileposts along the way, you know that your spiritual advisor will be checking with you each time you meet to see how you are progressing. Knowing that you must be accountable to your advisor motivates you to work harder, even when you are tempted to let your goals fall by the wayside. Your spiritual advisor's role in this area, however, is strongly influenced by whether or not you are a part of an accountability group.

Your Accountability Group

Many, if not most, American men operate in relative isolation. Following a model of self-reliance and self-sufficiency, we hurtle through life surrounded by many people but supported by few. All too often, we keep our peers at arm's length as we listen to the advice of the world: "Stand on your own two feet"; "Fend for yourself"; "Be a man." Implicit in these common exhortations is the notion that a "real man" does not need help from others.

Guided by this notion, we protect ourselves by hiding from the world's view the most significant aspects of our lives. The image of the iceberg has been widely used to illustrate this idea, which can be represented visually as follows:

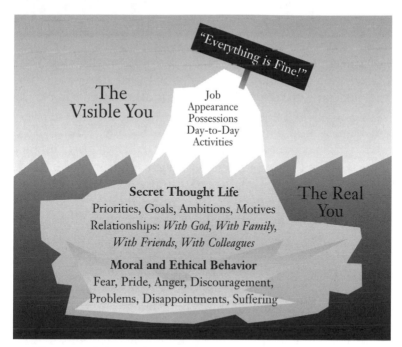

The tip of the iceberg is the part of yourself that you let the world see—your "best foot forward." But the part of the iceberg that lies beneath the surface is far larger than the part that pokes above. The lower portion can shipwreck you and the people you love if you don't let them know it is there. In his book *Character Counts*, Rod Handley has even called this the "Accountability Iceberg" because we are often dangerously unaccountable for the things below the waterline.[1]

Fortunately, God has a plan for helping us bring our inner lives into the light. "Let us consider how we may spur one another on toward love and good deeds," we read in Hebrews. "Let us not give up meeting together, as some are in the habit of doing, but let us encourage one another . . ." (10:24-25). God's Word instructs us to gather together with other Christians in order to encourage one another and hold one another accountable. Being part of an accountability group consisting of several of your peers is as important as meeting regularly with your spiritual advisor.

An accountability group is a group of men who meet regularly, usually weekly, to study the Word, pray together, and—most important—hold one another accountable to God's call. The emphasis on accountability makes it different from a fellowship group or a Bible-study group. To be part of an accountability group, a man has to be humble, open, willing to accept input, and eager to grow in the Lord.

Part of the reason that men's ministries such as Promise Keepers have experienced such phenomenal response in recent years is their fostering of the accountability group concept. Many local churches now have active men's ministries and even specific ministers who are devoted to pastoral care for the adult men in the congregation. These ministries are helping explode the myth that men cannot form close, meaningful bonds with other men.[2]

Although accountability groups are growing more and more common today, similar groups have existed for centuries. In the mid-1700s, John Wesley developed cell groups, which consisted of several Christian men and women who met together for mutual care and discipling. These cell groups called for a high level of accountability, as members were asked to honestly confess their faults and openly accept the observations and prayers of their fellow group members. Many of the guidelines followed by contemporary accountability groups are adapted from the model Wesley developed over two hundred years ago.

How does an accountability group work? Generally, at each meeting, every member has a chance to talk about his struggles and successes. The other members of the group listen supportively and nonjudgmentally, offering feedback, encouragement, and prayer. The group members hold one another accountable in specific areas of struggle by asking one another pointed questions. In *Character Counts*, Rod Handley identifies ten basic questions that an accountability group asks of its members at each meeting:

1. Have you spent daily time in Scriptures and in prayer?
2. Have you had any flirtatious or lustful attitudes, tempting thoughts, or exposed yourself to any inappropriate materials which would not glorify God?
3. Have you been completely above reproach in your financial dealings?
4. Have you spent quality relationship time with family and friends?
5. Have you done your 100% best in your job, school, etc.?
6. Have you told any half-truths or outright lies, putting yourself in a better light to those around you?
7. Have you shared the gospel with an unbeliever this week?
8. Have you taken care of your body through daily physical exercise and proper eating and sleeping habits?
9. Have you allowed any person or circumstance to rob you of your joy?
10. Have you lied to us on any of your answers today?[3]

Although not every accountability group will ask these questions in exactly the same way, every group should address the issues these questions raise. If you are struggling with any of these issues, answering such straightforward questions will not be easy; but in return for your complete honesty, you can expect unconditional support and respect.

Along with their agenda of honesty and sharing, most accountability groups have a formal or informal covenant that guarantees the supportive, affirming nature of the group. Men's-group members at Calvary Chapel in Denver, Colorado, offer a model with their "Koinonia Covenant":

1. The Covenant of Affirmation: "I will love you and affirm you no matter what you have said or done. I love you as you are for what Christ wants to make of you."
2. The Covenant of Availability: "Anything I have—time, energy, and resources—are all at your disposal. I give these to the group in a unique way."

3. The Covenant of Regularity: "I will give a regular part of my time to this group when it decides to meet. I will give that time priority on my schedule."
4. The Covenant of Prayer: "I promise to pray for you, to uphold you, and to attempt to be sensitive to the Holy Spirit concerning your needs."
5. The Covenant of Openness: "I will let you know who I am and where I am as a person in my hopes and hurts. I will need you!"
6. The Covenant of Honesty: "I will be honest in my feedback to you in what I sense and feel coming from you."
7. The Covenant of Confidentiality: "What goes on in this group stays here. I will say nothing that can be traced to my covenant partners."
8. The Covenant of Accountability: "You have the right to expect growth from me so that you may benefit from my gifts as I do yours. You have a right to ask me questions in that regard."[4]

As the members of a group learn to be honest with one another, they also learn that they share some of the same problems. They work together to meet their individual challenges, and they rejoice together in their individual successes. *Character Counts* points out that the end result of meaningful accountability group experience is growth in your Christian walk, deeper friendships, greater awareness, strengthening of your priorities, inner peace, and the development of a mutually beneficial support system.

Since the fall of 1985, it has been my privilege to be part of five accountability groups in different parts of the country. From these groups have come strong and lasting friendships. I have grown in my prayer life and in my study of the Word; and more often than I may have liked, my feet have been held to the fire by loving Christian brothers who love me too much to leave me the way I am. They refuse to let me be less than God wants me to be.

I recently had an informal reunion with five of my Cincinnati accountability group partners at the Promise Keepers conference in Cincinnati. Though it had been several years since I had seen them, we found that the bond we had formed in our accountability group was still strong. We have been blessed to be able to continue our friendship despite being geographically distant from one another.

Your Accountability Group and Your Spiritual Advisor

In many ways, an accountability group acts as an adjunct spiritual advisor. Your accountability group will nurture your spiritual growth, just as your spiritual advisor will hold you accountable. However, the advisor and the accountability group offer certain distinct services to you.

As a general rule, your spiritual advisor will be a man who is older or has been a Christian for longer than you. He will share with you the wisdom he has gained from many years of walking with the Lord, and the two of you will focus on your future: your spiritual goals and plans. Your spiritual advisor will offer specific direction and advice rather than simply listening to you and affirming you. In fact, your spiritual advisor may often do more talking than you do. He is a teacher and a guide.

By contrast, your accountability group will consist primarily of your peers. They will offer advice only when you ask for it, and they will listen to you and support you unconditionally. What teaching your fellow group members do will be through sharing their own experiences. Because the group exists for the purpose of holding its members accountable, the group's focus will be on the present and the recent past rather than the future.

As I have opened myself to the blessings of both a spiritual advisor and an accountability group, I have experienced the love of God manifested tangibly, through the love and care of my brothers in Christ. God's Word has come alive for me, I have seen my prayers answered, and I have been keenly aware of God's guidance for my life. My prayer for you is that you will experience the same blessings by sharing your Christian walk with the wise teachers and fellow pilgrims God has placed in your life.

NOTES

1. Rod Handley, *Character Counts: Who's Counting Yours?* (Grand Island, Neb.: Cross Training Publishing, 1995), 50.
2. If your church does not already have accountability groups, you might talk with your pastor about starting one of your own. Christian bookstores offer many excellent planning books and discussion guides for starting or leading small groups. One of the best resources for men's groups is Geoff Gorsuch's book *Brothers! Calling Men into Vital Relationships* (Colorado Springs: NavPress, 1994).
3. Handley, *Character Counts*, 60-61.
4. Gorsuch, *Brothers! Calling Men into Vital Relationships*, 50-51.

Chapter Two

YOUR CAREER MENTOR

You then, my son, be strong in the grace that is in Christ Jesus. And the things you have heard me say in the presence of many witnesses entrust to reliable men who will also be qualified to teach others.   (2 Timothy 2:1-2)

The single most effective way to build greatness into the lives of others—or have greatness built into your own life—is through the process of mentoring. In his excellent book *Mentoring: The Strategy of the Master*, Ron Lee Davis points out that "over half of all Nobel prize winners were once apprenticed to other Nobel laureates."[1] This suggests that *greatness*, however we choose to define it, can be taught and *is* taught through a deliberate "process of opening our lives to others, of sharing our lives with others; a process of living for the next generation."[2]

The Biblical Model of Mentoring

The best example of mentoring was provided by our Lord Jesus Christ. With the simple command "Follow Me," Jesus altered the course of history. Ron Davis writes that although Jesus "preached to the masses, he invested himself in a few, knowing that those few would invest themselves in still others, and thus transform the world."[3]

From Jesus' model we learn that mentoring is much more

than simply teaching, giving advice, counseling, or being a friend. Mentoring is a lifelong commitment to another individual, wherein the mentor shares his or her life with another with the intent of helping that person become all God wants him or her to be.

The Bible provides us with a variety of other mentoring models: Moses mentored Joshua in the art of leadership; Naomi was a mentor to Ruth, passing on to Ruth what she herself had learned about building and providing for a family; Barnabas mentored Paul by introducing him to the fledgling Christian church and taking him on missionary journeys; and Paul, in turn, mentored Timothy in church leadership and missionary work.

Mentoring, as it is modeled in the Bible, is an ongoing process of passing on knowledge to a new generation, though this process may occur in several different spheres. Just as in biblical times, today there are many types of mentors. Your spiritual advisor may become a type of mentor in matters of faith and spiritual practice. Your father or mother may be a mentor to you regarding family matters. In this chapter we are going to focus specifically on your career mentor: a professional in your field who, as Barnabas did for Paul and Paul did for Timothy, will help you succeed in your vocational call.

A Personal Model of Mentoring

I grew up with limited access to natural leaders around me: only partial access to my dad, no brothers, and few adult men who would take a genuine interest in my personal growth. But as I have grown older, God in His grace has *filled* my life with mentors. At the university, Simon exemplified the Christian lifestyle, Brad taught me excellence, Ralph shared unconditional friendship, and Bob taught me perseverance. These great friends helped show me what it means to be a man of integrity.

Through church and in seminary, God again graciously provided me with a team of mentors: Jerry taught me about righteousness, Ron shared a unique—and often hilarious—perspective on Scripture, Alice taught me how to blend academics and preaching, Dr. Taylor showed me how to be a pastor as well as how to preach, Dick taught me about financial stewardship in the church, Gary showed me how Christian counseling can work for the advancement of the Kingdom, Dr. Gillespie taught me how to love an imperfect church, Steve and Tony were always there with their prayers and personal support, and many others contributed to my personal development over the years. I thank God for all these mentors, and I pray that these blessings will always continue.

When I think of all the mentors God has blessed me with, one stands out specifically in relation to my career. Ned Patrick took me under his wing as I was just beginning my career in the life insurance business, and it was because of his leadership, example, and genuine interest in me that I became successful in that business.

I became acquainted with Ned through his son Pat, who was my best friend until he died tragically of malignant melanoma at the age of twenty-six. Ned owned a successful life insurance firm in Omaha, Nebraska, and I joined that firm a few years out of college. Although Ned had had a difficult childhood, had run away from home at an early age, and had made his way in business largely on his own, he understood the importance of investing himself in the lives of the young men whom he recruited to join his firm. He mentored all the young men who came into his business, teaching them the technical aspects of the insurance business and passing on to them what he had learned through his own experiences. We met with Ned on a regular basis in formal sessions designed for this purpose.

Ned's mentoring relationship with me, however, deepened

in a more informal, unstructured manner. I was often working in the office on Saturday mornings, and I can still smell Ned's pipe smoke from the many times he would invite me into his office to talk about my progress in my career, my goals, my dreams, and my family. In turn, he would share with me his background, his philosophy of business and of life, and his wit. During the seventeen years I worked with and for Ned, he became like a father to me, and he began to regard me almost as another son. After I moved away from Omaha, we kept up our relationship through frequent notes, phone calls, and visits.

The Qualities of a Mentor

Although Ned probably never thought of himself as a mentor in any formal sense, he exemplified the essential qualities of a mentor in all that he did. He was one of the rare few who can be truly excellent mentors. Ron Davis notes that among all the successful, capable people in the world, "there are just a handful who are willing to share their *lives*, who are willing to be transparent, vulnerable and open about their successes and their failures, their joys and their pain, their faith and their doubts." Worldly success and professional competence aside, "What ultimately determines the effectiveness of the mentoring process is not a person's style or skills or temperament, but a person's character, commitment, and love."[4]

Above all, a mentor is loving. Unfortunately, the word *love* is so often used to describe so many different actions and emotions that simply saying that a mentor is loving may not be saying much at all. But I want to look at the way a mentor loves the people he or she mentors by examining the qualities of a mentor's love as Ned expressed them to me. A mentor's love encompasses the qualities of *availability*, *openness*, *directness*, *nurture*, *respect*, and *credibility*.

Availability

To be a mentor, one must invest substantial time in another person's life. In our busy, fast-paced society, a mentor pauses to unselfishly give his or her time to others. Even as a mentor keeps up with the quick pace of business, he or she must constantly seek a balance between productivity and flexibility, leaving time for unplanned, unexpected challenges.

In my early days in the life insurance business, I knew that my boss was busy with responsibilities of his own, but Ned always made time for me when I needed his guidance or instruction. He never made me feel as if my questions were an inconvenience. Rather, he assured me with his welcoming smile and his open door that he was there to help me. Mentoring was not an interruption but an integral part of what Ned did.

Openness

A mentor is intensely interested in the life of the people he or she mentors and encourages them to talk about themselves. At the same time, a good mentor knows that personal sharing is a dialogue—not a monologue. Your career mentor opens up his or her life and shares it with you.

One reason I felt so comfortable going to Ned with difficulties in my career and my personal life is that Ned never portrayed himself as perfect or infallible. He told me about his mistakes and failures as well as his achievements and successes. He shared his hurts and disappointments with me and invited me to share my own. I was able to learn from his mistakes, and I was comforted to know that he was just as human as I was.

Directness

Although I knew that Ned was human and that he would not jump all over me for my mistakes, I also knew that when I went to him with a problem he would provide me with much more than a sympathetic ear. Ned never hesitated to tell me what I was doing wrong and point me in the right direction. Like any good mentor, he said what he meant. As a headstrong young man, I sometimes found Ned's directness hard to accept, but as I matured in my career, I learned to appreciate and accept it rather than reacting defensively.

A mentor tempers his or her directness, never criticizing harshly or squelching the creativity of the people he or she mentors, but offering direction with an attitude of respect and compassion. Ned would never tell me that I was messing up without talking with me about why I had approached a problem a certain way and helping me discover a better solution. Rather than saying, "Don't be stupid! Stop what you're doing and do it my way," Ned would say, "Gary, there's a better way to do this. Let's talk about it."

Nurture

I could accept Ned's directness because I knew that he offered his guidance out of love and concern for me. Moreover, I knew that my performance was key to the success of Ned's business and that Ned had a personal interest in seeing that I did my job well. By being available, open, and direct with me, Ned nurtured the best in me.

Your career mentor motivates you to do your best and excel in your career. He or she takes a genuine interest in you and deliberately sets aside time to teach you, share with you, and listen to you. In Ned's formal teaching sessions, he taught us the concepts, guidelines, and practices that were foundational to the business of life insurance. We learned more from Ned's wealth of experience and personal study than we could ever have learned simply from books or instructional manuals. Ned nurtured in us some of his passion for the business by helping us see that selling life insurance was not just about making money or building a business but also about helping people provide for their families and their businesses.

In the process of nurturing your growth in your career, your career mentor will inevitably nurture your personal growth as well. During those informal, one-on-one Saturday-morning sessions with Ned, I learned about dedication, integrity, loyalty, and strength of character. As I got to know Ned, I clearly saw that the traits that made him an honorable man were the same traits that made him successful in his business.

Respect

Perhaps the greatest part of a mentor's love is respect. Your career mentor sees and appreciates what you are currently achieving and recognizes your potential for achieving even more. Your mentor respects you and loves you because he or she sees in you all that God created you to be.

A mentoring relationship without respect will do more harm than good. I have known men whose mentors have been jealous of their success and have even begun working against them as they have grown more capable and confident in their own careers. Such mentors are really not mentors at all, for a true mentor's greatest satisfaction comes from watching the people he or she has nurtured grow and flourish. Mentoring should not be about ego but about serving. Mentoring at its best is done quietly, consistently, and behind the scenes.

Ned knew that he had more experience and expertise in the life insurance business than did any of his "new recruits," but he also knew that the young men who joined his business brought with them some excellent new ideas and energy. He never disrespected our youth or squelched our creativity by trying to make us into little replicas of himself. Instead, he gave us the general background we needed and then challenged us to bring our own unique style and strengths to the tasks before us. He respected us and valued the contributions we made to his business.

Credibility

Your career mentor actively loves and nurtures you by respecting you and being direct, open, and available to you. Your mentor deliberately teaches, instructs, and guides you. But your mentor will probably make the most profound impact upon your life when he or she isn't even trying to be a mentor. You will learn from your mentor primarily by watching him or her in action. People learn by example far more effectively than we learn by instruction. Consequently, credibility is an essential trait of any good mentor.

None of Ned's words would have sunk in if I had not seen him living and working in accordance with the instruction and guidance he gave me. Fortunately, one of the most important ways Ned nurtured my career was by his own example. As I watched him do business, I saw that he was a professional in every sense of the word: he was honest, diligent, competent, and caring; and he constantly strove to do better. He could not have nurtured these qualities in me if he had not possessed them himself—in full measure. A mentor earns credibility by practicing the principles he or she preaches.

Mentoring: A Lifelong Process

As I grew older and more experienced in my career, I never outgrew the need for a mentor. Ned was pleased to see me become more independent, and he gave me more and more responsibility to encourage my professional growth. Your relationship with your career mentor, though it will surely change over the years, may well last a lifetime.

Ron Davis traces the growth in the mentoring relationship between Barnabas and Paul, noting that although "the writer of Acts first refers to this dynamic duo as 'Barnabas and Saul [Paul],' . . . when you get to Acts 13, a significant reversal takes place. The writer no longer refers to 'Barnabas

and Paul' but to 'Paul and Barnabas.'" Having been men
tored by Barnabas, Paul went on to become the most dynam
ic and effective missionary Christ's church has ever known.
"What happened?" Ron Davis asks.

Did Paul shove Barnabas out of the limelight? No, Barnabas,
the Son of Encouragement, wanted it this way. He said, in
effect, "I believe in you, Paul. I want to help you, and in this
transition time I want to decrease so that you and the gifts
God has given you may increase."

This is a beautiful process of biblical mentoring . . . :
    Step 1: "I minister, you watch."
    Step 2: "We minister together."
    Step 3: "You minister, I watch."
    Step 4: "You find another to minister with and to mentor."[5]

As Ron Davis points out, mentoring is "a process of living
for the next generation." Just as your career mentor invests
in you, as you mature in your career, you may invest in oth
ers. One of the greatest ways you can return the favor your
mentor has done for you is to become a mentor yourself.

Following Ned's example, I became a mentor to Tom
Wilkinson, a young man who joined Ned's firm after I had
been there for many years. That man is now running the
business Ned started over forty years ago. Although Ned has
died, the principles on which he founded his business are still
being passed on through a continual process of mentoring.

Finding a Mentor

If you do not already have a mentor to nurture you in your
professional career, there are few things you can do that will
be of greater benefit to you than actively seeking a mentor.

After I relocated my business from Omaha to Cincinnati,
I continued to rely on Ned for his friendship and profes

sional advice, but I also sought out additional mentors to help me in my new ventures. When I initially started my own business, I went to ten men whom I considered to be leaders in the community and asked them if they would be willing to share with me the secrets of their success. They agreed; and they shared the stories of their failures as well, which turned out to be of particular value. It took a little over six months to get appointments with these ten leaders, but the education I received was absolutely invaluable. Some thirty years later, some of those men still track my career and continue to support my development.

The highest compliment you can pay someone is to ask him or her for advice. Jesus said, "For everyone who asks receives; he who seeks finds" (Matt. 7:8). In James we read, "If any of you lacks wisdom, he should ask God, who gives generously to all without finding fault, and it will be given to him" (James 1:5). God often provides the wisdom we seek through the counsel of a caring mentor.

Every professional man needs to ask God's guidance in selecting a career mentor. Ask God to direct you to a potential mentor, then go to that person humbly and ask if he is willing to provide you with ongoing personal leadership, wisdom, and counsel. You can't force a person to be your mentor, but if you keep seeking, you will find the person God wants to be your mentor. When God is in the process, the results can be truly amazing!

NOTES

1. Ron Lee Davis, *Mentoring: The Strategy of the Master* (Nashville: Thomas Nelson, 1991), 19.
2. Ibid., 16.
3. Ibid., 21.
4. Ibid., 22-23.
5. Ibid., 44.

Chapter Three

YOUR FINANCIAL PLANNER

"Do not store up for yourselves treasures on earth, where moth and rust destroy, and where thieves break in and steal. But store up for yourselves treasures in heaven, where moth and rust do not destroy, and where thieves do not break in and steal. For where your treasure is, there your heart will be also."   (Matthew 6:19-21)

The Bible is very clear in its teaching about money. Both the Old Testament and the New Testament teach that "the love of money is a root of all kinds of evil. Some people, eager for money, have wandered from the faith and pierced themselves with many griefs" (1 Tim. 6:10). The Gospels tell the contrasting stories of Zacchaeus, who found joy when he repented of his greed and gave his possessions to the poor, and the rich young ruler, who turned away from Jesus sadly when asked to give up his riches.

How we handle the resources God blesses us with is a matter of no small interest to God. Our material resources are not really ours at all. God is grieved, and we rob ourselves of our joy, when we hoard possessions and personal wealth. Everything we have belongs to God, and we have the responsibility to manage our money wisely and give generously.

Your financial planner can help you do just that.

What Is a Financial Planner?

Your financial planner is responsible for helping you frame the "big picture." This advisor talks with you about all the aspects of your finances—your income, your necessary monthly expenditures, your spending habits, your savings and investments, your future plans and needs, your insurance coverage—and helps you put those pieces together into a unified whole.

If you do not already have a financial planner, ask for referrals from friends and colleagues. You may try calling several and talking with them briefly about your resources and your goals. Your financial planner should have either a Chartered Financial Consultant (ChFC) or Certified Financial Planner (CFP) designation. The American College (P.O. Box 1513, Bryn Mawr, PA 19010, telephone: 215-526-2500) can furnish you with a list of Chartered Financial Consultants in your area.

As the person who helps you bring the various aspects of your finances together, one of the financial planner's primary roles is to provide you with referrals to other consultants and specialists in the fields of insurance, investments, accounting, and so forth. Although some financial planners may also sell insurance or investment products, many serve only as consultants and work on a fee-only basis. Working with a network of financial professionals, the financial planner serves as the quarterback of the planning process. He or she helps you articulate your objectives and then directs you to the professionals who can provide you with the products to help you achieve these goals.

Goals and Financial Planning

What are your financial goals? Your financial planner can help you take a long view of your finances and start working toward your long term goals. These goals may include the following:

- paying for college or vocational school for you, your spouse, or your children;
- paying off your home mortgage;
- owning your own business;
- funding your retirement;
- giving to your church or other charitable organizations.

Without the help of a financial planner, meeting these goals may seem like an impossible dream. If you are like most people, you have probably often felt that you have too much month at the end of your money. But with proper planning, you can pay your bills *and* meet your long-term goals.

Setting goals is an essential part of the financial planning process. In that process, we need to seek God's guidance and commit our goals to God. In Proverbs we read,

> All a man's ways seem innocent to him,
> but motives are weighed by the LORD.
> Commit to the LORD whatever you do,
> and your plans will succeed.
> . . . .
> In his heart a man plans his course,
> but the LORD determines his steps.
> (Prov. 16:2-3, 9)

Plans that have developed in our hearts and minds as we have been open to the nudging of the Holy Spirit, plans that we have prayerfully committed to God, are bound to succeed—in God's way and on God's timetable. Plans that we make according to our own selfish desires and without regard to God's will for our lives are bound to fail.

Values and Financial Planning

Because your financial advisor will play such a pivotal role on your advisory team, you should make a special effort to find an advisor who is a Christian. When your advisor is seeking to help you set goals and make decisions in accordance with God's will for your life, you reap a double blessing. However, as I said in the introduction, I know it is not always possible to find a professional advisor who is also a committed Christian. If the most professionally competent financial advisor you can find is not a Christian, don't rule out the possibility of working with him or her; but be certain that you always keep your Christian values and beliefs about money at the forefront of your goal-setting and decision-making process.

The world tells us to consume, consume, consume. When we turn on the television, listen to the radio, or read the newspaper, we are constantly bombarded by the message, "You are what you buy." It is easy to be persuaded by this message and to become preoccupied with gaining more material possessions. I have often felt the pressure to spend money on things I know I don't need: a newer, faster, flashier car; more expensive, more luxurious vacations; state-of-the-art sports equipment. But I have learned that buying into the consumer mentality—trying to "keep up with the Joneses"—only creates more anxiety for me.

Fortunately, there is a cure for the consumer mentality and the anxiety it causes. Jesus explained the cure in his Sermon on the Mount:

> So do not worry, saying, "What shall we eat?" or "What shall we drink?" or "What shall we wear?" For the pagans run after all these things, and your heavenly Father knows that you need them. But seek first his kingdom and his righteousness, and all these things will be given to you as well. (Matt. 6:31-33)

Financial planning is a matter of trust and priorities. When we take God at His word and put God first in our lives, we realize the folly of worrying about possessions. God will provide for our needs. He may not grant us our every whim and desire, but we can trust God to provide us with the things we truly need. All we have to do is trust God and be good stewards of the resources He provides.

If you find that, despite your hard work and genuine effort, you are unable to earn enough money to meet your and your family's basic needs, you probably need to seriously redesign your way of managing your money. Depending on your situation, you may benefit from the services of a consumer credit counselor or a career counselor.

Before you can maximize the benefit of the services of a financial planner, you must be committed to responsible financial management. Make this a priority. Freeing yourself from debt or from the consumer mentality frees you from crippling financial worry and enables you to serve God with your whole life. If you follow one simple principle, you will be free of debt and free from the consumer mentality more quickly than you can imagine: *spend less than you earn.* It is possible to follow this principle no matter how much or how little you earn, but it may require some very creative financial planning and some initially difficult sacrifices on your part.

When you have freed yourself of debt and conquered the consumer mentality, you can do your best work with a financial planner; but your Christian values must remain an integral part of your relationship with this advisor. In setting financial goals and working toward achieving those goals, remember that everything you have belongs to God. We are not to be possessed by the goods of this world or to seek more possessions simply for our own pleasure. Rather, we are called to be good stewards, to provide for our families, and to contribute the firstfruits of our labors to God's work on earth.

Planning to Give

Perhaps the most important part of your financial planner's job is to help you give the resources God blesses you with back to God. Scripture says,

> Honor the LORD from your wealth,
> And from the first of all your produce;
> So your barns will be filled with plenty,
> And your vats will overflow with new wine.
> (Prov. 3:9-10 NASB)

How many of us give "from the first of all [our] produce"? At a minimum, as Christians we are called to tithe of our resources. Traditionally, this means giving 10 percent of our income to support the work of the Kingdom. If you do not already tithe, 10 percent of your income may seem like a lot to ask. But as you begin the spiritual discipline of tithing (or if you already do tithe), you will learn that it is not a burden but a blessing. "Give, and it will be given to you," Jesus says. "A good measure, pressed down, shaken together and running over, will be poured into your lap. For with the measure you use, it will be measured to you" (Luke 6:38). In fact, one of the greatest blessings of working with a financial planner is that it may enable you to contribute far more than your tithe to the ongoing work of God's Kingdom.

Beyond tithing, your financial planner can help you follow Scripture's instruction regarding the management of your financial resources in many ways. I would like to briefly discuss a few of these: *bequests, gift annuities, perpetuation of gift contracts, charitable remainder trusts,* and *pooled income funds.*

One of the simplest ways to make a significant contribution to your church or to another charitable organization is by making a *bequest* in your will. Your financial planner and your attorney can help you incorporate into your will provisions for certain funds or properties to be donated to the charitable organization of your choice at the time of your death. The items designated in this bequest will be excluded from federal estate tax calculations on your estate, and the designated resources will be donated to your church or other organization. (See figure 1.)

Figure 1. BEQUEST

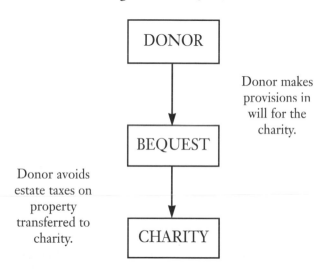

A *gift annuity* is an excellent way to donate funds to your church or other charitable organization and continue to receive income from those funds while you are alive. Your financial planner can show you how to make a gift of property to your church while preserving a portion of that gift to continue generating income for you. For example, if you would like to give a large monetary gift to your church, you may give that money now by depositing it in an annuity managed by a bank, insurance firm, or other financial institution. The principal will belong to your church, but you may continue to receive the interest earned on the principal during your lifetime. At the time of your death, your church may choose to leave the principal alone and simply receive interest payments, or it may choose to spend or reinvest your gift. (See figure 2.)

Figure 2. GIFT ANNUITY

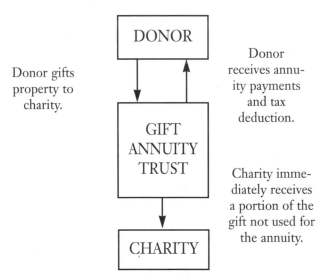

In order to set up a *perpetuation of gift contract*, your financial planner will need to work in tandem with your life insurance advisor (see chapter 4). Let's say, for example, that you currently give $10,000 per year to a certain charitable organization. Without proper planning, at the time of your death these regular contributions will cease.

However, for a relatively small cost to you, you can purchase a perpetuation-of-gift life insurance contract with $100,000 worth of coverage and designate the charitable organization as the beneficiary. You may deduct from your taxes as a current gift whatever premiums you pay for this insurance contract as long as this contract is owned by the charity. At the time of your death, $100,000 passes tax-free to the charity and is excluded from your estate. The charity then receives the $100,000 (tax-free), which, if set aside in an investment vehicle that produces 10 percent annual interest, perpetuates your $10,000 annual gift forever! (See figure 3.)

Figure 3. PERPETUATION OF GIFT

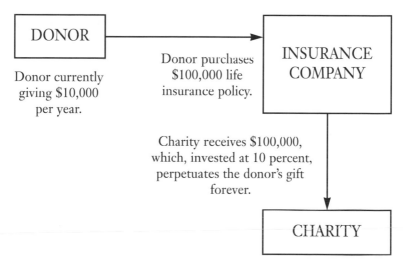

Charitable remainder trusts are extremely effective and increasingly popular planned giving tools because, like gift annuity accounts, they provide income to the donor during his or her lifetime and provide a significant gift to a church or other charitable organization at the time of the donor's death. Your financial planner and your attorney can help you set up a charitable remainder trust and deposit gifts of property (such as stocks, bonds, real estate, and business interests) into that trust. You receive a tax deduction based on the assets you deposit in the charitable remainder trust. The assets in the trust technically belong to the trust; but during your lifetime, the income earned by the assets may be paid to you and your spouse. At the time of your death, the proceeds of the trust are redirected toward the organization you have designated as the beneficiary of the trust. (See figure 4.)

Figure 4. CHARITABLE REMAINDER TRUST

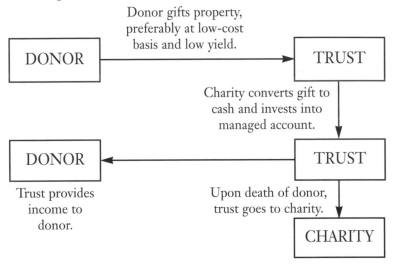

There are several types of charitable trusts: for example, the charitable remainder unitrust with a wealth replacement trust, which uses a life insurance contract to provide benefits of the trust to both the charitable organization and the surviving members of the donor's family at the time of the donor's death. (See figure 5.) Your financial planner can direct you toward the type of trust that is best for you.

Figure 5. CHARITABLE REMAINDER UNITRUST WITH WEALTH REPLACEMENT TRUST

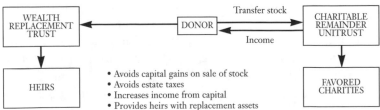

Even if your resources are limited and your estate quite small, you can contribute to the work of God's Kingdom. A *pooled income fund* is designed for donors who want to add muscle to a relatively small donation. This fund pools the resources of several donors and manages them together in order to maximize the investments and minimize investment costs.

To give to a charitable organization through a pooled income fund, you make a gift of property to a fund that also receives contributions from several other similar donors. In return, you receive annual income from the fund based on your ownership of shares in that fund, as well as a current tax deduction. At the time of your death, your contribution to the fund is removed from your estate tax calculations, thus lowering the taxes levied on your estate; and your share of the pooled income fund passes to the charitable organization you have designated. (See figure 6.)

Figure 6. POOLED INCOME FUND

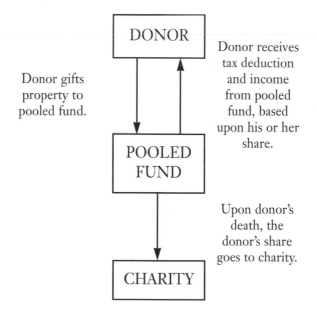

DONOR

Donor gifts property to pooled fund.

Donor receives tax deduction and income from pooled fund, based upon his or her share.

POOLED FUND

Upon donor's death, the donor's share goes to charity.

CHARITY

These are just a few of the ways a financial planner can help you make the most of your money for the good of God's Kingdom. When you begin to see your resources going to work for the Kingdom, giving back to God will become a source of great joy and satisfaction to you.

With proper planning, you can legally and morally *decrease* the amount of money you pay to income tax and estate taxes and *increase* the amount you are able to contribute to your church and other charitable organizations. This is a great blessing to you and to the organizations you support.

If your gift or estate is particularly large, you will probably want to consult with a charitable gift planner. Charitable gift planning is a specialized type of financial planning. This person will have experience in helping donors and recipient institutions plan substantial gifts. He or she can help you maximize your gift.

Whatever your financial situation, proper planning with the help of a caring, competent professional is an essential step toward putting your finances in proper perspective. By working with you to set priorities and goals, helping you free yourself of debt and the consumer mentality, and helping you give back to God, your financial planner enables you to put your treasure where your heart is.

Chapter Four

YOUR INSURANCE ADVISORS

"Who of you by worrying can add a single hour to his life?"
(Matthew 6:27)

It may seem unusual to begin our discussion of the insurance advisors' role in the personal advisory team with Jesus' teaching about not worrying. How can a man think about preparing for the unexpected without being anxious? In Matthew's Gospel, Jesus tells his disciples to "see how the lilies of the field grow. They do not labor or spin. Yet I tell you that not even Solomon in all his splendor was dressed like one of these. If that is how God clothes the grass of the field, which is here today and tomorrow is thrown into the fire, will he not much more clothe you, O you of little faith?" (Matt. 6:28-30).

In truth, Jesus' teachings in this area are extremely pertinent. Jesus is talking about trust. As complicated as our lives can be, as pressing as our responsibilities often are, many of us forget to trust God to provide.

The Life Insurance Underwriter

Some men put off investing in life insurance—because they are unfamiliar with the coverage available, because they are not comfortable thinking about their own mortality, or because they are not thinking realistically about the unexpected financial hardship their death might cause their families. But if we listen to what Jesus says, we understand that God will provide for us. Responsibly preparing for the time when the Lord calls us to heaven is another way of being a good steward of the resources God has blessed us with.

By seeking out a skilled life insurance underwriter and building a strong relationship with him or her, you are saying, in effect, "God, I trust your timing, and I trust you to provide for me and my family, even if you should call me home tomorrow. I'll do my part to take care of the resources you provide."

Most men's greatest financial resource is their future income stream. Financial plans of all types hinge on our ability to produce income. Consequently, it is important to decide what percentage of your income stream you want to protect for your spouse, your children, your business partners, and your charities in the event of your death. That great American philosopher Will Rogers once joked about an Oklahoma neighbor of his who had died with minimal life insurance: "He must not plan on being gone very long!"

As more and more people have recognized the vital importance of properly protecting their families, the life insurance industry has become a significant business on the American economic landscape. The array of coverage available to you may seem overwhelming, but this is no reason to put off acquiring adequate life insurance. Indeed, properly designed life insurance contracts are the cornerstone of any effective financial plan. A good life insurance underwriter can guide you through the complexities of buying adequate life insurance and, in the process, become your friend, confidante, and highly trusted advisor.

As you work through the issues surrounding providing protection for your loved ones, your life insurance advisor will get to know you, your family, and your business very well. The more honest you are with this advisor, and the more personal background you share with him or her, the better he or she will understand who you are and what you are trying to accomplish for those you are trying to protect. Use this advisor as a critical resource in the process of creating and properly structuring your estate.

Choosing the Right Personal Life Insurance

There are many different types of life insurance contracts. First, there are *level premium contracts*. For these, you pay the same amount of premium each year. Also known as *permanent contracts*, these do not have arbitrary expiration dates, and you can own them for as long as you wish. Second, there are *term insurance contracts*, which cover you for a specific term—a predetermined period of time—and then expire on a given date. Additionally, there are contracts that increase in premiums and benefits and contracts that decrease in premiums and benefits.

Many employers offer their employees group life insurance at little or no cost to the employee. Group policies typically contain a *multiple-of-income factor*. For example, if you earn $40,000 per year, you might have $80,000 or $120,000 in group insurance benefits, payable to a beneficiary you choose. You may also choose to purchase *accidental coverage* on yourself, so that if you should die by other than natural causes, your family has an added level of financial protection. These group policies are an excellent benefit, and you should take advantage of them if your employer offers them to you; but by themselves they will probably not be adequate to provide for your family in the event of your unexpected death.

Few insurance companies can be all things to all people. Most companies offer a handful of products that represent what they do best. For example, some companies specialize in high-quality, universal life contracts (a blend of interest-sensitive permanent insurance and term insurance). Some companies specialize in whole life (or permanent) products.

Some companies specialize in term insurance products. Some companies specialize in disability income products (a *critical* product for protecting your income stream). Your life insurance advisor is your guide through what can seem like a labyrinth of insurance contracts and companies. Together, you can match the needs of your family and business with the various insurance products available to you.

The first step in choosing the right life insurance is evaluating your needs. In the personal insurance arena, people implement coverage for the following reasons:

- to preserve a portion of their income stream for their surviving family members;
- to take care of expenses associated with their death;
- to pay off home mortgages;
- to fund vocational training or college education for their children;
- to help fund retirement;
- to pass on financial resources for those ministries or charities they support.

Another important reason for implementing life insurance coverage, whether personal or business-related, is the issue of estate taxes. If you develop a significant estate in the United States, you also develop a federal estate tax liability. Tax liabilities follow ownership. At the time of your death, all of the assets in your estate are totaled up, and then a federal tax table is applied to them. Depending upon the size of your estate, more than half can go to the federal government!

The Lord said, "Give to Caesar what is Caesar's, and to God what is God's" (Matt. 22:21). God calls us to pay our fair share of taxes, and that is as it should be. However, we are not called to have our estates wiped out by taxes because of ignorance or neglect.

The beauty of using insurance proceeds to pay estate tax liabilities is that the estate can use "discounted dollars," as opposed to the net dollars from the estate itself. Keep in mind that every "net dollar" in an estate has *already* been taxed by the government. If federal estate taxes are also levied on that dollar, you can literally end up paying some 80 to 90 percent of your estate to taxes! But if, after you use all available legal vehicles to reduce your taxes, you use insurance dollars to pay remaining federal estate tax liabilities, you will lose far less to taxes.

If your estate is substantial, you and your insurance advisor should explore the issue of estate taxes in depth. You may structure your contract in such a way that you pay a premium to fund estate tax liabilities. Such coverage costs literally pennies on the tax dollar—hence the term "discounted dollars."

Keep in mind that a properly designed life insurance contract can be an excellent way to pass on resources to support your church and other organizations. Ask your life insurance advisor about setting up a charitable remainder trust or a perpetuation-of-gift contract. These tools help you minimize your estate taxes and maximize the resources you are able to pass on for the work of God's Kingdom. (Charitable remainder trusts and perpetuation-of-gift contracts are discussed in more detail in chapter 3, "Your Financial Planner.")

Though there are some similarities in everybody's situations, no one's financial situation is exactly like yours, and your life insurance underwriter needs to help you evaluate your needs and design a customized plan to protect the people and organizations you care about.

Choosing the Right Business Life Insurance

If you are involved in a business partnership, your advisor should be knowledgeable about "key man" insurance, for partners in a business whose success depends on the continued involvement of both partners, and "cross purchase" coverage, which enables partner A to buy out partner B's stock in the business in the event of partner B's death.

Your advisor may also recommend deferred compensation coverage, a method whereby some current income is channeled into a life insurance contract that provides benefits to the business or family in the event of your unexpected death. While the policyholder is alive, the contract builds up significant funds that can be used as supplemental dollars for retirement.

Split-dollar coverage may also be an effective planning tool. In this type of coverage, the premium cost is split between the business and the executive. With proper planning by your life insurance underwriter and your accountant, this type of coverage can often be designed in such a way that there is virtually no cost to you.

These are just a few of the benefits you should explore with your life insurance advisor if you own a business. As you can see, whether your estate is made up primarily of personal assets (not primary stock ownership in a business) or business assets, the process of purchasing adequate life insurance may involve complex decisions. The most important choice you will make about your life insurance, however, is your choice of a life insurance advisor.

Choosing the Right Life Insurance Advisor

Because your decisions in this area directly affect your loved ones and your ability to pass on the financial resources God entrusts to you, it is extremely important that you seek out a life insurance advisor who is professional, experienced, and competent.

In order to qualify for life insurance, you must show "insurable interest." In other words, you must prove that you have a valid and legitimate reason for acquiring the insurance. You must pass a physical exam and meet the moral and financial requirements of a particular insurance carrier. The larger the amount of insurance you request, the more rigorous and detailed the underwriting process will be. You need a competent person working on your behalf as the liaison to the insurance company. Your life underwriter must be able to present your needs and your situation in an accurate and favorable light to the insurance company.

Just as you need an advisor who will represent you in the best possible light to the insurance carrier, you need a trustworthy advisor who represents solid and reputable companies.

There is a wide range of competency among insurance companies. Among the abundance of products available to you, there is a significant difference in the "net cost" of your insurance product. Net cost is measured by the difference between the premiums you pay into a contract and the cash value and dividends you create within that contract (assuming it is a permanent and not a term insurance contract). A competent life insurance underwriter should help you avoid products that require a high premium but create small value. He or she should help you understand the appropriate numbers on insurance contracts and guide you to a *quality* insurance carrier.

The A. M. Best Company produces detailed annual reports on the quality of the insurance products offered by various carriers in the industry. Ask your life insurance underwriter to share that information with you.

Although you may have no particular interest in the amount of business your life insurance underwriter produces, the economic reality is that he or she must produce sufficient business in order to support himself or herself. That's true for every businessperson! You can learn a lot about your life insurance underwriter's competency by finding out how much business he or she generates.

It bodes well for you if your life insurance underwriter is

a member of the Million Dollar Round Table, is a member of a local association of life insurance underwriters, and has a Chartered Life Underwriter (CLU) designation issued by the American College in Bryn Mawr, Pennsylvania. You should seek referrals from professionals in your community as you search for the proper advisor. Be assured that the attorneys, accountants, and trust officers in your community know who the top underwriters are. You certainly don't have to "let your fingers do the walking" to find one!

In addition to professional competency, you should look for personal compatibility with your life insurance advisor. It is easy to see how a life insurance advisor who knows you and your family well, who cares about you, and who shares or at least understands your values and religious convictions will do a better job for you than will an advisor with whom you have a strictly professional relationship. Professional competency is priority one, but if possible, seek out an advisor who is a Christian and a potential friend.

If you choose the right life insurance underwriter, he or she will become a vital member of your personal advisory team. When the Lord does finally call you home, it is your life insurance underwriter's job to be the bridge between your family and the various insurance carriers who cover you. Your underwriter can bring a personal perspective to the job of properly distributing funds in accordance with the terms of your insurance contracts.

The Casualty Insurance Underwriter

Many of the same principles that apply to life insurance also apply to casualty insurance. This includes automobile insurance, home insurance, medical insurance, and fire insurance. Responsibly insuring our cars, homes, and businesses is another way of working with God to be a good steward of the resources God provides.

Even more than when shopping for life insurance, we may be tempted to do without sound advice from a trusted advisor when purchasing casualty insurance. But if you simply trust the Yellow Pages, the Internet, or the advertisements of the largest casualty insurance carriers with your decisions regarding casualty insurance, you may find that you make some costly mistakes. When the time comes for you to use your insurance, you may even find that you are not covered as well as you thought you were. Do not minimize the importance of finding a competent, caring professional to advise you in your casualty insurance needs.

When looking for a casualty insurance advisor, don't look only at the size of the agency he or she works for. Larger companies, naturally, have larger advertising budgets, and consequently some of them are household names. But remember that just because you know their name doesn't mean that they offer competitive products. Some smaller, less well-known companies have excellent products. Rather than letting size and image be the determining factors in your choice of a casualty insurance carrier, ask your advisor for reports that measure and rate the quality of casualty insurance companies and their products.

Just as important as the quality of products offered by a carrier is the quality of *service* offered by your casualty insurance agent. Look for someone who shows a genuine interest in your well-being. When you are doing business with this agent, ask yourself whether you are being treated with respect and concern, or merely as a source of business. If you've ever tried to decipher your policy and make sense of your benefits, you'll appreciate the importance of having an advisor who will take the time to go through your policy with you and make sure you know exactly what your policy covers and how to use it.

If your current agent is not willing or able to do this, consider changing agents or even carriers. Your effort to find a good advisor will more than pay for itself in the long run.

A good agent and advisor will help you measure your needs in each of the areas that you need to insure and then act as your guide through the extensive supply of products available in order to be certain you select the best policies for your situation. The agent can put his or her expertise to work for you, evaluating the amount of protection you need, the amount of deductible you should pay, the insurance company or companies you use, your cost, and your method of payment. No cookie-cutter policy can provide the level of coverage that a customized insurance plan developed by a competent advisor can.

After you have developed a plan and implemented coverage, you should be sure to review your policies periodically with your advisor. If your assets increase or your liabilities decrease, share this information with your casualty insurance advisor. It is this advisor's job to continually monitor your needs and make sure that your customized protection is adequate.

Keeping up an active dialogue with a trusted casualty insurance advisor will cost you far less, in the long term, than simply making a one-time decision and hoping for the best as your circumstances change. Select a quality casualty insurance agent and then grow with him or her.

Buying life or casualty insurance does not imply that we do not trust God to provide for us; rather, it demonstrates that we are faithfully doing our part to take care of what God does provide. Your insurance advisors can help you responsibly care for yourself, your family, and your business.

Chapter Five

YOUR ACCOUNTANT

I have learned to be content whatever the circumstances.
(Philippians 4:11)

In his letter to the Philippian church, the apostle Paul exemplifies the Christian attitude toward material possessions. In thanking the Philippians for their generosity in providing for his needs, he writes, "I know what it is to be in need, and I know what it is to have plenty. I have learned the secret of being content in any and every situation, whether well fed or hungry, whether living in plenty or in want" (Phil. 4:12).

Paul knew how to be content with very little or with great abundance because he had learned to be a good steward. He recognized that he did not own anything and that all his material blessings and provisions came from God. We can deduce that Paul did not gather material possessions to himself or spend money frivolously. He lived within his means, knowing that he could not serve God if he were preoccupied with money.

The same goes for us. If we are preoccupied with our desire for more money; if we spend more than we earn and fail to give back to God; if we do not manage our financial resources properly, we are not able to serve God with our whole lives.

Whether your finances are very simple or very complex or

somewhere in between, a certified public accountant (CPA) can help you manage them properly.

Your Accounting Needs

Many men think that they have little or no need for a professional accountant, except, perhaps, at tax time. The fact is that seeing an accountant three or four times a year is helpful even for men whose finances are very simple. Certainly, having your taxes done correctly is important. The tax laws in our country change virtually every year, and unless you deal with them on a regular basis (as your accountant surely does), it is practically impossible to keep up with them all. Your accountant will keep you accurate while protecting you from paying more than you should.

In addition to helping you with your taxes, your accountant can advise you in many matters: What is the best way to fund your children's education? Would it be to your advantage to prepay the mortgage on your home? Should you invest in a personal or corporate pension plan? Should you invest in an IRA, a 401K, or a 403B plan, and if so, how much? How will your investments affect the amount of taxes you owe? Your accountant can help you answer each of these questions.

Over the course of my career, my financial compensation has varied greatly. For many years, I earned a significant income in the corporate world; for a few years, I earned nothing at all as a full-time, adult student; for the past several years I have worked in full-time Christian ministry, where my financial rewards are outweighed by my sense of satisfaction and purpose in following God's call for my life. Based on my own experience, I can assure you that no matter how much or how little money you earn, God will provide for your needs. Furthermore, with the help of a good accountant who truly understands your situation, you can maximize your resources and find ways to save and invest for your future.

Values and Accounting

When you are selecting an accountant, it is important that you make your priorities clear concerning your money. Though accountants are often quiet, low-key folks, they should also be good listeners and good communicators. I recommend discussing, early in your relationship with your accountant, the issue of tithing. Malachi 3:10 says, " 'Bring the whole tithe into the storehouse, that there may be food in my house. Test me in this,' says the LORD Almighty, 'and see if I will not throw open the floodgates of heaven and pour out so much blessing that you will not have room enough for it.' " God asks us to trust Him enough to tithe— to take at least 10 percent of our resources and return them to God.

The practice of tithing is a spiritual act of obedience and trust; God is more concerned about our obedience and trust than about our money. In Psalms, we hear God say,

"For every wild animal of the forest is mine,
   the cattle on a thousand hills.
I know all the birds of the air,
   and all that moves in the field is mine.
If I were hungry, I would not tell you,
   for the world and all that is in it is mine.
. . . .
Offer to God a sacrifice of thanksgiving."
                    (Ps. 50:10-12, 14 NRSV)

We know that everything belongs to God. The question is, What are we going to do with those assets God has put under our care? When we generously give back to God, we grow spiritually. Moreover, our giving enables the work of the Kingdom to go forward.

Your accountant's role on the advisory team is central. He or she will work with the other financial professionals on your team to make sure your money is directed as you wish it to be. Don't leave giving out of that process! Whether you already have significant savings or are just beginning to put some money aside, you should work together with your accountant and your financial planner to see that you spend, save, invest, and give your money in such a way as to provide for yourself and your family, prepare for your future, and contribute to the work of God's Kingdom. Your accountant will help you be a good steward of the resources God provides.

Chapter Six

YOUR INVESTMENT ADVISOR

"Well done . . . ! You have been faithful with a few things; I will put you in charge of many things. Come and share your master's happiness!"　　　　　(Matthew 25:21)

In Matthew's Gospel, Jesus tells a parable about a wealthy master who entrusts his slaves with large sums of money before going on a journey. When the master returns from his journey, he is delighted to learn that two of his slaves have wisely traded with the money entrusted them and have doubled their holdings. But with the one slave who has hoarded the money entrusted to him, the master is extremely angry.

The Spirituality of Investing

God has blessed each of us with resources and abilities, and God expects us to invest what we are given wisely. When we jealously hoard God's gifts or go about investing them with a greedy and ungrateful attitude, we are forgetting that they are not really ours at all. Investing our money in things such as property, stocks, and bonds can be a way of giving back to God. As our investments grow, we are better able to take care of ourselves and our families, and we are better able to share the gifts God has given us.

In the area of financial investments, we need an advisor

who understands the solid spiritual foundations of investing as well as he or she understands the fluctuations of the world of commerce.

What Is an Investment Advisor?

An investment advisor is a financial professional who earns his or her living by researching investment products such as stocks, bonds, money market accounts, and mutual funds; discerning which products can best serve his or her clients; and then selling these products. Although they are often called investment brokers, the term *advisor* is a more accurate description of their role. Your investment advisor may serve as the broker through whom you will purchase investment products, but he or she is responsible for much more than completing a financial transaction.

Your investment advisor has the responsibility of helping you safeguard or maximize your investments. It is this advisor's job to help you clarify and understand your investment goals. Building an advisory relationship with your investment broker is important, for someone who knows you well and shares your spiritual values will be able to help you think through and verbalize what you want to accomplish through your investments.

If you don't know where to look for an investment advisor, you may try calling several and talking with them briefly about your resources and your goals. Many excellent advisors work for small firms as well as for large firms such as Fidelity, Dean Witter, Merrill Lynch, Prudential Bache, and Salomon Smith Barney. As with all the professional advisors, the best way to find the right advisor for you is through referrals, initial meetings or interviews, and observation.

You do not have to be fabulously wealthy to begin investing. In fact, most people begin by investing a small amount and then adding to the investment over a period of years. A good investment advisor will be glad to work with you regardless of the amount of your initial investment, because he or she knows that a small but consistent investment grows exponentially over time.

Risk and Investing

Because the process of investing can be highly technical, your investment advisor needs to be well-educated in his or her field. The stock market is a place of great opportunity, but it can also be a place of great risk. A competent advisor can help you minimize your risk and can also help you measure your risk tolerance.

A young couple investing for retirement can tolerate more risk than, for example, a retired couple living on a fixed income. Even if a high-risk investment in stocks or mutual funds performs poorly for a year or two, it will probably rebound and turn a good profit before the younger investors are ready to cash it in. With most investments, the higher the risk, the higher the potential reward; the lower the risk, the lower the potential reward. Your investment advisor should know you well enough to understand your comfort with financial risk, your goals for your investments, and when you plan on using the money your investments earn.

Depending on your investment goals, you may choose short-term, medium-term, or long-term investments. For example, you may want to invest money for two years or less in order to buy a new car. For such a short-term goal, you and your investment advisor will probably choose a low-risk investment such as a money-market fund or certificate of deposit. Perhaps you are recently married and you and your spouse want to invest for five years in order to put a down payment on a house as you start a family. A medium-term investment such as this one may call for an investment with more potential for growth (and thus higher risk). If you are investing for your children's college education in fifteen years, or investing for your own retirement, your investment advisor will probably encourage you to consider long-term, moderate-risk, high-growth-potential investments such as stocks and mutual funds.

Lately, there has been much conversation in the investment business about firms that charge a commission on the sale of investment products versus firms that charge "no commission." Some brokerage firms advertise that they charge no commission and suggest that you get more for your money by avoiding the commission. The fact of the matter is that every business must pay its electricity bill and other overhead costs, and the investment business is no exception. One way or another, you will pay an investment broker for services provided, so don't worry too much about whether your payment is identified as a commission, a fee, or some other cost. When selecting an investment advisor, an investment firm, or a particular investment product, look at the net results the advisor, firm, or product achieves after all the expenses (whatever they happen to be called) are paid. It is fair that you should pay for the expertise of an investment broker, and consequently you have a right to expect excellent service and results.

There are so many investment products available, and so many different reasons for investing, that it can seem intimidating or overwhelming. Finding a well-educated, well-informed, caring advisor to help you make good investment decisions will save you a lot of stress, confusion, and costly mistakes.

The Goals of Investing

Some Christian men are uneasy with the idea of investing. For some, the word *invest* conjures up images of money-hungry Wall Street brokers in designer suits, willing to go to any length, forsake any principle, and neglect any relationship in order to make a dollar. Surely this is not what God wants! Didn't Jesus tell the rich young ruler to "go, sell your possessions and give to the poor"? Indeed, and when the rich man turned away from Jesus because he couldn't part with his property, Jesus continued, "I tell you the truth, it is hard for a rich man to enter the kingdom of heaven. Again I tell you, it is easier for a camel to go through the eye of a needle than for a rich man to enter the kingdom of God" (Matt. 19:21, 23-24).

Note that these words from Jesus were directed very specifically to a man who was too attached to his material possessions; and remember the parable with which we began this chapter. In that parable, the master commends the slaves who wisely invest the money he has entrusted them with. God has blessed us with gifts, and God expects us to be good stewards; but we don't *own* anything! Everything belongs to God.

As Christians, we have two basic goals for our investments: (1) to use the resources God has blessed us with in order to care for ourselves and our families, and (2) to use our God-given resources in order to give back to God. When you look for an investment advisor, look for someone who believes in these goals and will not be focused exclusively on accumulating wealth.

Without question, your investment advisor should be daily (often on a minute-by-minute basis) connected to the world of finance. He or she should know the state of the market and be able to help you make financially savvy decisions. When you hear about a promising potential investment through business acquaintances, television programs, the radio, the newspaper, or the Internet, you should be able to count on your advisor to give you even more thorough information and advice. Furthermore, your advisor can bring a levelheaded, logical, relatively dispassionate perspective to the investment process and help you guard against becoming emotionally wedded to a stock.

Most good investment brokers possess these qualities, but not all investment brokers will understand and sympathize with your unique goals for your investments—particularly your goal of giving back to God. In selecting your investment advisor (and all your financial advisors), make certain that he or she understands that giving back to God is a priority for you.

As you build a relationship with your investment advisor, and as you see your investments grow, you may find that you are able to return much more than 10 percent to God. Giving to your church and to other Christian ministries will become a great joy for you and your family.

Investing is an area where the rubber hits the road for the Christian man. As the saying goes, "If you show me a man's checkbook and his calendar, I will show you his heart!" In financial affairs, our trust in God (or lack of it) becomes very apparent. Will God bless this or that investment? We don't know for certain. But in faith, we know that we need to make the best decisions we possibly can, with the help of a caring, competent investment advisor.

Chapter Seven

YOUR ATTORNEY

Those who forsake the law praise the wicked,
but those who keep the law resist them.
Evil men do not understand justice,
but those who seek the LORD understand it fully.
(Proverbs 28:4-5)

n ancient Israel, God's law and the law of the nation-state were one and the same; religious authorities were also political authorities. By the time of Jesus, the Israelites were governed by the Roman Empire, and so they had two sets of laws to follow. Among the early Christians there was considerable confusion over the issue of earthly versus heavenly authority, but Paul instructed Christians to obey the earthly authorities as representatives of God's authority. "Let every person be subject to the governing authorities; for there is no authority except from God, and those authorities that exist have been instituted by God" (Rom. 13:1 NRSV).

Today, the laws of our country are numerous and complex; but as Christians, we are called to conscientiously obey them. In most matters, if we follow the Ten Commandments in both letter and spirit, we will have no fear of transgressing the laws of our nation and our state. But in some technical matters, we need the guidance of an expert in the law in order to make certain we are faithful to God's call.

In addition to helping you understand and adhere to federal and state law, your attorney can help you protect the resources God entrusts to you.

Your Attorney's Role on the Advisory Team

Your attorney is an anchor of your advisory team because he frequently interacts with each of the other advisors. You've heard the saying "All roads lead to Rome"; but in business, some say that "all roads lead to the attorney's office." At those points where the law intersects your life, there is often a need for a legal document. Your attorney will probably interact with your other advisors in the areas of real estate, insurance, accounting, financial planning, investments, trusts, and medicine, to name a few. For example:

- your real estate advisor may call on your attorney to evaluate contracts and taxes and liens relative to the sale and purchase of real estate property;
- your investment advisor may work with your attorney to help work out beneficial interests of investment plans and see that an estate plan is properly carried out;
- your attorney may consult with you and your doctor to draft documents stating your wishes concerning long-term treatment and medical care;
- your casualty insurance agents may call on your attorney to represent you in court following an automobile accident;
- your attorney may work with your financial planner in drafting your estate plan, your will, and other documents relating to your financial resources.

Because so many areas of your life call for legal counsel, your other advisors will expect you to include an attorney on your advisory team.

Professional Competence

"Do-it-yourself" kits for various legal proceedings are becoming increasingly common. These kits come with fill-in-the-blank forms and instructions to help you do everything from composing your own will to processing your own divorce. Unfortunately, doing your own legal planning (unless you are an attorney) is like giving yourself a haircut: it can be done, but the result is usually less than desirable. A stack of forms and a booklet of instructions are no replacement for a qualified attorney. In legal matters of any complexity (and most legal matters are complex), you need the advice and assistance of a living, breathing *person*.

There is no easy way to become an attorney. It requires four years of undergraduate study, followed by the rigors of law school (usually three additional years). After completing law school, one must pass the Bar exam, and then often serve as an apprentice or clerk. Early years of practice usually demand long hours of research and "grunt work." By the time attorneys become partners in a firm or have private practices, they have paid their dues many times over.

Nonetheless, not all attorneys are equally competent. In order to find the right attorney for you, you'll have to do some research yourself. Ask other professionals in your community for recommendations and referrals. Then ask the attorneys themselves if they have experience handling the type of work you need done. You may sit down and talk with several attorneys before you find the one who will be able to serve you best.

Personal Compatibility

When we think of the traits that make a good attorney, we often think first of presentation and speaking skills. These are important, but even more important is the attorney's ability to *listen*. Your attorney needs to hear—*really* hear—your plans for your family, your business, and your estate. Your attorney needs to get to know you and other members of your family. He or she needs to listen to what you say and then ask meaningful questions in order to fully understand your legal needs.

Working with your attorney is all about communication. Your attorney has the legal expertise to put your wishes into action, but he or she must first take the time to fully understand your wishes. As the "drafter of documents," your attorney takes your hopes, dreams, and plans and puts them down on paper. In the process, you will be challenged to think through and evaluate your goals.

It is imperative that you select an attorney you trust. The attorney is responsible for helping you meet federal and state legal requirements regarding important personal matters, *not* for helping you circumvent the law. If you sense that your attorney is constantly looking for loopholes and shortcuts, prayerfully consider finding an attorney who is more concerned with keeping your personal and business matters well within the law.

Your Will or Estate Plan

One area where most men will need an attorney is in drafting the legal documents that become the foundation of their estate. After listening carefully and intentionally to you, your attorney will be able to serve you by drafting thorough, customized estate papers. Depending on your financial situation, your legal documents may be very simple or very complex. For most men, legal planning becomes progressively more complex as the years go by.

The documents your attorney drafts should reflect *your* desires. An attorney who doesn't know how to listen properly may do little more than make minor changes to a one-size-fits-all will or estate plan. This is of little more help to you than a do-it-yourself kit. Undoubtedly, you will want advice and guidance from your attorney; but by the same token, you do not want to be coerced into accepting a legal plan that doesn't do what you want it to. Work closely with your attorney to see that the documents drafted for you are effective instruments for accomplishing your plans for your family, your estate, and your business.

Wherever you live in the United States, if you die without a will (the technical term for which is *intestate*), the state in which you reside will apply a standardized ("boilerplate") will to your estate, no matter how large or small your estate may be. Unfortunately, when it comes to wills, one size does not fit all. The state's boilerplate will is better than no will at all, but it will not function in the way you would choose. The administrative costs of probating your estate will be significantly increased, and the assets of your estate will be under the jurisdiction of the state courts for what can seem to your survivors like an interminable period.

Clearly, failing to draft a will with a qualified attorney could cause genuine hardship for your surviving family members. Do *not* leave your family adrift without a proper will, trust, estate plan, or whatever legal plan is appropriate for your circumstances. If you do not have a current will, I urge you on behalf of your family and your business associates, do not hesitate any longer to call an attorney and start the process.

At the time of your death, there will be myriad tasks to be attended to. In his book *Beyond Survival*, Léon Danco writes, "If the successful business[owner] . . . does not have the courage to face the problems of the future, then his banker and attorney will do it for him on the way back from his funeral—four cars back from the flowers."[1] His warning is blunt but true.

However, if you have prepared properly, your family will be able to handle the necessary tasks with a minimum of procedural trouble. Your attorney will wear many hats on your behalf, and competence is critical for the well-being of your wife, your children, and your business associates. He or she will answer dozens of questions from all directions and assist your family in handling the nitty-gritty tasks that must be done. If you have taken the time to let your attorney get to know you and your family, your attorney can also serve as a confidante and comforter during this difficult time.

If you wish to pass on some of your financial resources to support the work of the church or other charitable organizations, you will need to enlist the assistance of many members of your personal advisory team. Your attorney is particularly central to this process. Believing that we have a responsibility to maximize our own resources for the work of God's Kingdom, my wife and I recently completed and updated our own wills and estate plan. Our attorney helped us make provisions for a portion of our estate to go to Kingdom work. After taxes and administrative costs, the remainder of our estate will be divided up, exactly as we wish it to be, among our children and grandchildren. Creative planning with our attorney has allowed us to direct our resources exactly as we believe—after much prayer and consideration—God would have us do.

Witnessing Is a Two-Way Street

In all your dealings with your personal advisory team, you will have the opportunity to share your Christian beliefs and your experience of God. When you are dealing with important areas of your life, this type of witnessing comes naturally. However, witnessing is a two-way street. In my own life, I have been richly blessed by the Christian witness of two of my attorneys.

Long before I became a Christian, I was powerfully influenced by the witness of my attorney Joe Byrne. Joe's love for the Lord and his dedication to his church was clearly manifested in all that he did. His quiet, thoughtful, and sensitive witness to me helped plant a seed that would be nurtured by many others along the way before I finally accepted the love of God into my life.

Later, the Lord used another attorney, Bob Marriott, to help bring me into the Kingdom. Bob's subtle and adroit use of Scripture in business settings fascinated me. I remember on several occasions asking Bob where he found the wisdom he shared in our legal dealings. In response, he would turn to the Bible and share with me a passage that related perfectly to the situation at hand. I was amazed that, even higher than his technical mastery of the law, Bob treasured the Word of God. God's Word *never* comes back void!

My experiences with these attorneys, as well as with many other of my personal advisors, taught me that I do not need to compartmentalize my life into categories of spiritual and secular. This is one of the greatest rewards of building a personal advisory team. As you build your own advisory team, you will find that you gain much more than financial security or business knowledge. Your advisory team will help you integrate your spiritual life with your life in the world.

NOTE

1. Léon A. Danco, *Beyond Survival* (New York: Prentice Hall, 1975), viii.

Chapter Eight

YOUR DOCTOR

Do you not know that your body is a temple of the Holy Spirit, who is in you, whom you have received from God? You are not your own. (1 Corinthians 6:19)

Scripture tells us that our bodies are the residences of the Holy Spirit! Therefore, good health is not only a blessing but also a responsibility. We honor the Holy Spirit by eating right, staying in shape, and seeing our doctor regularly. If we neglect our health, we dishonor the Holy Spirit. Does this mean that when we suffer from a disease or a disability we are neglecting the Holy Spirit? Absolutely not. But it does mean that God expects us to do everything we can to keep our bodies in their best possible state of health.

Staying healthy does not come naturally to everyone. Few of us can always resist the lure of junk food or the temptation to "veg out" instead of working out. Developing a healthy lifestyle is an intentional process, and one of the most important parts of the process is selecting a quality physician.

Choosing a Credible Doctor

Your physician will become a primary advisor concerning this vital area of your life, so it is important to find a physician who is credible. A doctor who practices what he or she preaches will have a strong and positive influence on your own health decisions. For example, if you are trying to lose weight, a doctor who eats well, exercises, and maintains a healthy body weight will be more helpful to you than a doctor who does not eat a well-balanced diet and who chooses not to exercise. Likewise, a physician who smokes will have no credibility when he or she encourages you to quit.

When I was thirty-five, I injured my ankle playing basketball. My doctor told me that I should put the ankle in a metal brace and not exercise it for six weeks. I'm not a doctor, but I felt that six weeks of having my ankle muscles locked in a brace and not exercised would do my ankle more harm than good. I feared it would adversely affect my walking gait, would rule out running, and would create an imbalance throughout my entire body. I also feared that my ankle muscles would severely atrophy and I might lose my ability to play sports or even be active. Looking back on that experience, I see that the doctor's recommendation was a result of his own sedentary lifestyle. Following his advice might have been extremely detrimental to my health.

I went to see another doctor for a second opinion. On this doctor's recommendation, I went through physical therapy. I soon regained regular use of my ankle and immediately changed doctors. The first doctor lost his credibility with me when I realized that, as a person who was not physically active, he could not provide the best diagnosis and treatment for someone who was.

It is through experiences such as this one that we can discern our doctors' technical competency. Don't be afraid to get a second opinion if you are inclined to doubt your doctor's advice. Even in the world of HMOs and preferred providers, you have a degree of choice, so exercise it! Your effort to find the right doctor is always worthwhile.

Making Time for Health

Many men have a tendency to take inappropriate pride in saying, "It's been five years since I saw the doctor." Whether because we think we're too busy or because we think we are too healthy, many of us neglect regular visits to the doctor. If you are priding yourself on how long it has been since you've been to the doctor, you are practicing a type of false economy. Whatever time or money you may save can be more than offset by the physical and financial cost of an illness or disease that gets a foothold while you are away from the care and observation of your physician.

Even if you don't like to see a doctor, do so! You have a moral obligation to those you love to stay in good health. God gave us these marvelous bodies in which we reside for a reason, and being good stewards means taking care of those bodies. If you take the Bible seriously when it says that you are a temple of the Holy Spirit, you will find time in your schedule, no matter how busy you may be, to attend to your health.

As you grow older, periodical, thorough health evaluations become even more vital. A yearly or twice-yearly visit to your doctor gives your doctor the chance to monitor your long-term health patterns. Many diseases, including cancer, can be successfully treated if they are detected early. If you put off seeing your doctor until you notice disturbing or debilitating symptoms, you may allow a disease to develop past the point of treatment.

Even if you are in excellent health, there are manifold benefits of seeing a physician on a regular basis. Several weeks ago, I went to my doctor for a thorough annual exam. We looked at my blood pressure, pulse, cholesterol level, weight, exercise patterns, sleeping patterns, eating patterns, and other vital signs. Although I keep in good shape by exercising regularly, I know that I need to change my eating patterns. My doctor affirmed this and gave me specific guidance, recommending that I take in more juices, fruits, and vegetables and fewer meat and dairy products. His recommendations were not highly technical; in fact, the healthy eating habits he recommended were matters of common sense. But having the affirmation, endorsement, and support of my doctor in my efforts gave them a stamp of credibility that motivated me to do what I know I should do anyway.

There is an old joke that we hope the doctor will tell us we are "in good condition for the condition we are in." I must confess that when I go in for annual physical checkups, I do so with a mixture of anticipation and apprehension. I appreciate my doctor's positive feedback for the things that I am doing well, but I am always afraid that he may discover something that falls into the category of bad news. I must continually remind myself that detecting something such as high blood pressure or a malignant tumor early is far better than letting it go unnoticed and untreated. With this in mind, I push through whatever discomfort I feel about setting up my physical exams.

On several different occasions through the years, my dermatologist has spotted and surgically corrected a melanoma spot (skin cancer), which resulted from overexposure to the sun when I was a boy. Although undergoing the minor surgery was a bit scary at the time, it prevented a serious, long-term problem.

I have stayed physically active through running and playing basketball and tennis. Consequently, I have had my share of injured ankles, shoulders, fingers, and calves. Through proper medical treatment from a competent, caring physician—and through physical therapy when appropriate—I have been able to maintain my flexibility, good health, and ability to stay active.

As the years go by (I am now in my sixties), I have learned that I have to be increasingly intentional about exercising. It is so easy to neglect exercise for a day or two, and a day or two can then easily stretch into a week or two. The longer one is sedentary, the more painful it is to get back in shape, so the less likely one is to do so. If you deliberately select a doctor who values physical exercise (and, preferably, is physically active), your doctor can help keep you accountable in this area.

Choosing a Caring Doctor

We value doctors for their technical competency, but almost as important is their bedside manner. Many doctors, in order to protect their emotions, put a wall around their feelings so that they can deal with patients on a strictly professional level. When my wife's father died, the doctor delivered the message with all the sensitivity of a sledgehammer. The information he delivered was technically accurate, but the manner in which he delivered it was absolutely devastating to our family.

However, many other doctors are willing to invest themselves more deeply in the lives of their patients. These doctors have realized that healing is not only a physical process but also a mental, spiritual, and emotional journey. When you are selecting a doctor, look for a real professional who is responsive to *every* aspect of healing.

Dr. William Haynes' superb book, *A Physician's Witness to the Power of Shared Prayer*, discusses in depth the spiritual aspect of healing. Haynes writes:

> I wore my white coat, stood alongside the hospital bed, rarely touched a patient except for the examination required in the routine physical, and undoubtedly talked more than I listened to what my patients were struggling to tell me concerning their private lives, which was often the real cause of the "disease."
>
> . . . I was basically a "zipped-up" professional, both unable and unwilling to open my heart and "take off the white coat" in order to enter into what was troubling the patient's soul.[1]

Haynes goes on to quote another doctor, who writes, "You [the doctor] may not wish it, but some of your patients regard you as their pastor or priest. A discreet sharing of your wounds—your views of life and death, courage and faith, and joy and tragedy—may be very appropriate."[2]

Dr. Haynes points out that the gap between the hurting patient and the caring physician is, unfortunately, getting wider and wider. He shares a conversation he heard between two medical students at the hospital: " 'Why bother listening to the details of the heart murmur when an echocardiogram with Doppler will give the answer?" one [student] asked his classmate. In other words, why touch the patient with a stethoscope when a bioengineering tool can be used? Why take a medical history from a patient personally, when a computer can take the history?"[3] Sadly, our medical schools sometimes help widen the gap between patient and physician.

The good news is that it doesn't have to be that way. It shouldn't be that way! Dr. Haynes is just one of the growing number of doctors who recognize the need to bridge the gap and strengthen the relationship between patient and doctor. Clearly, your doctor plays a key role in bridging the gap; but don't forget that *you*, as the patient, are also responsible for building the doctor-patient relationship. If you want to include your doctor in your personal advisory team, you can't keep him or her at arm's length. Inform your doctor about your lifestyle, about your physical and mental stresses, and about your health concerns.

Prayer and Healing

Healing, as we have seen, is as much a spiritual process as it is a physical one. You will benefit greatly if you find a doctor who is courageous enough to bring his or her spirituality into the medical practice.

Scripture says to us, "Pray continually; give thanks in all circumstances, for this is God's will for you in Christ Jesus" (1 Thess. 5:17-18). Both doctors and patients are called to pray continually. For each of us, doctors included, taking our professional roles out of the world and into the Word is no small task. William Haynes is one doctor who has accomplished this task. He writes that bringing prayer into his practice of medicine "took great courage on my part. . . . I had never encountered a course in medical school that mentioned the spiritual nature of a patient."[4]

As he began to think about the spiritual aspect of medical practice, Dr. Haynes learned that he needed to be sensitive to the unspoken prayers of his patients as well as the prayers they shared with him. The patient's prayer "may be audible, accompanied by a touch or a hug, or may be totally inaudible. . . . Many times when praying with people you have only to ask the Holy Spirit to speak the words through you, and the Spirit will give you the words of comfort that the patient needs. To my constant amazement, the words are always right on target—just what was needed, not too much or too little."[5]

Dr. Haynes shares that after praying with his patients he has seen expressions of great relief. "The patient's usual response has been a deep sigh, some tears or outright crying (frequently joined by me), and a visible lifting of the burden as the patient hands this burden over to God."[6] In praying with his patients, Dr. Haynes often reaches out to them with a compassionate touch. "Touch has a healing power in its own right," he writes. "Through the laying on of hands we become more visible and perhaps more effective as channels for God's healing love, and grace."[7]

By joining the power of prayer with his own medical expertise, Dr. Haynes has seen remarkable results. As an experienced and successful doctor, Haynes has shown that there need not be any rift between science and spirit. His personal, spiritual approach to medicine puts to rest the notion that the doctor-patient relationship should be entirely clinical.

Jesus is the Great Physician, but he often chooses to do his healing work through vessels known as doctors and nurses. Your doctor, a key member of your personal advisory team, is a channel of God's love and care for you.

NOTES

1. William Haynes, Jr., *A Physician's Witness to the Power of Shared Prayer* (Chicago: Loyola University Press, 1990), 8.
2. Walter M. Benjamin, "Healing by the Fundamentals," *New England Journal of Medicine* 331 (1984): 597; quoted in Haynes, 14.
3. Haynes, *A Physician's Witness*, 94.
4. Ibid., 29.
5. Ibid., 30-31.
6. Ibid., 32.
7. Ibid., 39.

Chapter Nine

YOUR SECONDARY ADVISORS

*There are different kinds of gifts, but the same Spirit
...Now to each one the manifestation of the Spirit is
given for the common good.* (1 Corinthians 12:4, 7)

O ne of the great beauties and strengths of the Body of
Christ is that each member has his or her unique abilities, interests, and needs. When we Christians truly
act like the Body of Christ, we put our abilities and interests
to work in order to meet one another's needs.

Because every man's needs are unique, no two personal
advisory teams will look alike. While one man may have an
ongoing need for legal counsel, another man may call on an
attorney for the sole purpose of helping him draft his will.
While one man may trade actively on the stock market and
thus communicate with his investment advisor on a regular
basis, another might make only a few long-term investments
and thus speak with his investment advisor far less frequently. What is a primary advisor for one man may be a periph-
eral or secondary advisor for another.

By no means should you feel restricted by the basic design
this book lays out for a personal advisory team. I believe that
every mature Christian man will have some need for each of
the advisors I have discussed, but I know that not every advisor will be a primary member on every personal advisory
team. I also know that you may need to add to your team one

or more advisors whom I have not mentioned. The basic principle still applies: In every area of your life where you will need the ongoing services of a professional, seek the advice and counsel of a professional who cares about your well-being and with whom you can cultivate a personal advisory relationship. Depending on your situation, various financial and medical professionals may serve on your personal advisory team.

Secondary Financial Advisors

Among the secondary financial advisors whom you may call upon for ongoing professional advice are a Realtor, a trust officer, and a charitable giving advisor.

Your *Realtor* can help you make one of the most important decisions you will ever make regarding you and your family: purchasing a home. If you are a young man, perhaps recently married or just starting a family, you will probably want to purchase a home as quickly as possible in order to start building equity. Even if you think you can't afford a home right now, I recommend contacting a Realtor to discuss your situation. Be up front with your Realtor about your price range and your needs, but at the same time, don't be afraid to talk about your dream home and your long-term goals. A good Realtor can use this information to help you find a "starter home" in your price range. Your Realtor may suggest investing in a lower-priced home, living there for some time, saving and building equity, and then looking for your dream home a few years later. Your Realtor can also provide you with valuable information about the neighborhood: for example, whether the property values are likely to go up or down, the quality of the schools in the area, and the crime rate in the area.

If you already own a home, you may call on a Realtor when you want to sell your home and purchase a new one, or if you decide you would like to purchase land or an additional home as part of your investment portfolio. Again, your Realtor will be a valuable advisor, guiding you through this potentially complex investment decision.

If your financial assets are substantial, you may consider establishing a trust. A *trust officer* will be an essential part of this process. Your trust officer will work with your financial planner and your attorney to establish a trust into which certain assets of your estate will be deposited. He or she will see that your trust functions according to your wishes.

Commonly, the beneficiaries of trust funds are the children of the person establishing the trust. If your assets are significant, you can use a trust to pass them on to your children when they have reached an age when they are able to use the trust fund appropriately. In many cases, a trust owner (or "grantor") does not deposit assets into the trust during his or her lifetime. Usually, the "bucket" of the trust remains empty until the death of the grantor, and only then is it filled up with the assets of the estate.

Because your trust officer is the contact point between the beneficiaries of your trust (probably your children) and the financial institution that administers the funds, your trust officer becomes a very important person in the lives of your family. Consequently, you should choose your trust officer carefully, taking into consideration how well that person will be able to communicate and work with your children. If possible, arrange for your family members to meet and get to know your trust officer before your death and the implementation of the trust.

Your trust officer will serve your family after your death by supervising the investment of assets in the trust, preparing tax documents, keeping records, and performing other administrative functions. He or she will also work with other members of your advisory team, including your attorney, your accountant, your investment advisor, and your financial planner. The work your trust officer performs will be of great comfort—both financial and emotional—to the people you love. This advisor helps you continue providing for your family after you are gone.

A *charitable giving advisor* may serve as an adjunct to the financial planner. In chapter 3, "Your Financial Planner," we discussed some of the ways your financial planner can help you give more of the resources God has blessed you with back to God. Most financial planners should be very familiar with these giving tools, but some may not have been specially trained with this as their area of expertise. If your financial planner has not worked extensively with charitable giving techniques, you may need the services of another planner who is an expert in this area. The charitable giving advisor will be a specialist, perhaps working with a company, such as PhilanthroCorp, that exists solely for the purpose of coordinating major gifts from donors to charitable organizations. He or she can help you minimize your estate taxes and maximize the amount you are able to pass on to the work of the Kingdom by setting up a charitable remainder trust, a pooled income fund, a bequest, a gift annuity, or any combination of the many tools available to you for charitable giving.

Secondary Medical Advisors

In chapter 8, "Your Doctor," we discussed the importance of building a personal advisory relationship with your doctor or general practitioner. Over the course of your life, you will probably need to consult several medical specialists; and some of these may become part of your personal advisory team. These may include a chiropractor, a podiatrist, a dermatologist, a cardiologist, or others. Here, I will discuss two medical professionals that almost every man will need to see on a semiregular basis: your pharmacist and your pediatrician.

As simple as it seems, walking up to a *pharmacist*, extending your hand, and actually introducing yourself is a rarity today. Introducing yourself to your pharmacist, giving him or her some background information on you and your family, and stating that you intend to visit him or her for your medicinal needs will quickly elevate you beyond the level of "customer" and onto the level of "real person" in the eyes of your pharmacist.

Pharmacists invest their time and money in college and graduate school. They devote themselves to ongoing education about the medicines they recommend and dispense. They know their business, and most are interested in knowing their customers, as well.

If your pharmacist knows something about your medical history and the medications you take, he or she can be of great assistance to you. Your pharmacist can work with your doctor to prescribe the right medicine and the right dosage for what ails you. In some cases, your pharmacist's expertise and personal knowledge of you can steer you clear of potentially hazardous or even deadly side-effects of certain drugs and combinations of drugs. On a more basic level, establishing a friendly, personal relationship with your local pharmacist will make life easier and more pleasant for you when you are sick and in need of medication.

If you have children, it is imperative that you find a competent, caring *pediatrician* to attend to their medical needs. Both parents should meet with the pediatrician in person to discuss their children's medical history and needs.

Even more so than with adult practitioners, the pediatrician's bedside manner is a primary consideration. When you are selecting a pediatrician, ask yourself whether you think this doctor will take a genuine interest in your children's health. Will he or she communicate with your children on their level? Will he or she treat your children gently and with patience, taking into consideration the fear and discomfort many children feel when visiting the doctor? Is his or her office a welcoming, comforting place? If the answer to any of these questions is no, keep looking until you find a pediatrician with whom you can feel completely comfortable entrusting the healthcare of your children.

When you have found the right pediatrician, let your pediatrician know how much you value his or her services, and show your pediatrician the respect that doctor deserves. When you demonstrate that you take your child's health seriously, you raise your pediatrician's confidence level in you.

Parents are often inclined to worry excessively over minor injuries or illnesses, and sometimes we are even afraid to call the pediatrician because we fear he or she will tell us we are overreacting. However, it is always better to follow your instincts and consult your pediatrician rather than waiting around, hoping an injury will heal itself or an illness will pass. Establishing a personal relationship with your pediatrician will keep you from hesitating to call when you are concerned about your children's health.

A good pediatrician will appreciate your calls and take your concerns seriously. As you and your children get to know your pediatrician better, your pediatrician will be able to serve you better.

Your Informal Advisory Team

In this book I have discussed the advisory team as a somewhat formal cabinet of professionals whom you deliberately seek out and (in most cases) hire for their professional advice and counsel. Even your relationship with those team members who are not hired professionals (your career mentor and your spiritual advisor) will probably be somewhat formal and will certainly be deliberately, regularly maintained. The advisors I have included in my discussion of the personal advisory team will assist you in integrating your personal and spiritual life with some of the more technical aspects of your life—your financial, medical, and legal needs.

I have concentrated on these areas not because I think they are more important than other areas—such as your home life, your personal relationships, and your hobbies and interests—but because I know that these are the areas where most men need professional advice and assistance.

I began the book with my discussion of your spiritual advisor's role in the advisory team for a reason. This advisor will help you make the connections between your spiritual life and every other aspect of your life. In your relationships with all the other advisors, your primary goal should be to see that you are living the gospel in everything you do—including your financial dealings, your legal planning, and your care of your body.

The advisory team as I have described it in this book is a formal, deliberately gathered group of advisors; but in addition to this group, every Christian man has an informal advisory team consisting of friends, family members, colleagues, and acquaintances. Your father, mother, and other family members may advise you concerning family matters. As you learn from their strengths and experiences, your business colleagues may serve as adjunct career mentors. Friends and acquaintances may advise you in a variety of areas, including your health, your finances, your personal interests, and your spiritual life. You will surely receive valuable advice in spiritual matters from the members of your church.

Scripture tells us that every member of the Body of Christ has unique gifts and a unique contribution to make to all the members of the Body:

> There are different kinds of gifts, but the same Spirit.
> There are different kinds of service, but the same Lord.
> There are different kinds of working, but the same God

works all of them in all men. Now to each one the manifestation of the Spirit is given for the common good. (1 Cor. 12:4-7)

God has given each of us unique talents, abilities, and gifts with the expectation that we share them with—and accept them from—one another. In this sense, the entire body of believers is your personal advisory team. When we welcome the gifts that every member of the Body has to offer, we receive God's blessings in abundance.

CONCLUSION

Unless the LORD builds the house,
its builders labor in vain.

(Psalm 127:1*a*)

In everything we do, we should seek God's guidance and direction. God has a plan for each of our lives, and it is by living in accordance with God's plan that we experience God's joy and abundance. Building a personal advisory team takes time and effort on your part, but your labor will be richly rewarded if you commit it to the Lord.

As you begin to build your personal advisory team, may I suggest you bathe every step of the process in prayer. Pray for discernment and discretion in selecting your advisors. Pray that God will lead you to the best advisors. Pray for openness and honesty in your communication with your advisors. Pray that the advisors God wants for you will be open to God's will and will agree to serve as your advisors. Pray for God's guidance as you set goals and make plans regarding your spiritual life, your health, your career, your finances, and your legal needs; and pray that you will not lose sight of the goals and plans that God lays on your heart.

When Christians earnestly pray for God's guidance and then actively seek to live the gospel in all they do, remarkable things happen. "I can do all things through him who strengthens me," writes Paul in his letter to the Philippians (4:13 NRSV). Yet when we join with other believers to pray and act on God's will, God's power is manifested even more dramatically: "Again, I tell you that if two of you on earth agree about anything you ask for, it will be done for you by my Father in heaven. For where two or three come together in my name, there am I with them" (Matt. 18:19-20).

I have seen the truth of these scriptures played out dramatically again and again as I have helped people build and work with their own personal advisory teams. One man, an executive at a major corporation, had never taken the time to do any financial planning, though he had often felt the Holy Spirit's tug to make his money count for something bigger than himself. He confessed to me that part of the reason he had delayed in his planning was that he didn't know any financial professionals whom he could really trust. With prayer and determination he was able to assemble a personal advisory team that helped him coordinate a major gift of over ten million dollars, split among his church, his alma mater, and a charity. Thanks to some creative and careful planning with the help of his advisory team, this man's gift will continue to further the work of God's Kingdom for many years.

Another man, a hard-working and successful engineer, made coordinating a personal advisory team a high priority and saw the quality of his life improve dramatically as a result. He prayed consistently as he began building his team, and he followed God's leadership in choosing advisors whom he admired and liked on a personal as well as professional level. He even went so far as to meet together with all his advisors on a quarterly basis.

When his doctor and his spiritual advisor got to know each other and began talking together about this engineer, they realized that they shared many of the same concerns about him. They recognized some of the harmful patterns the man had established in his life; and they strongly urged him to reevaluate his priorities, advising him to travel less, sleep more, exercise regularly, eat better, spend more time with his family, and commit more time to the Lord.

The man valued the counsel of his advisors and acted on their suggestions. His advisors, in turn, helped him meet his goals by offering their knowledgeable, practical counsel. Today, the man is a happier and healthier person, a better husband and father, and a more deeply committed Christian than he had been prior to building his personal advisory team.

The value your personal advisory team brings to your life comes, not from the individual members of your team, but from the power of the Lord working in and through your relationships with your advisors.

My prayer for you is that you will open yourself to receiving the gifts God wishes to bless you with through your personal and professional relationships. Scripture promises—and experience bears out—that our lives improve for the benefit of ourselves, our families, our businesses, our churches, and God's Kingdom when we surround ourselves with and seek the counsel of a team of wise, caring, competent advisors.

APPENDIX
Professional Organizations

The following is a list of professional organizations that may assist you in finding qualified advisors by furnishing you with directories or referrals of professionals in your area.

The American College can provide information about Chartered Life Underwriters (CLUs) and Chartered Financial Consultants (ChFCs).

        address: P.O. Box 1513

                    Bryn Mawr, PA 19010

        phone: (215)526-2500

The *College of Financial Planning* can provide information about Certified Financial Planners (CFPs).

        address: 1700 Broadway

                    Suite 2100

                    Denver, CO 80290

        phone: (303)860-7500

        fax: (303)860-7388

The *American Institute of CPAs* can provide information about Certified Public Accountants (CPAs).

address:	1211 Avenue of the Americas
	New York, NY 10030-8775
phone:	(212)596-6200

The *National Association of CPCUs* can provide information about Chartered Property and Casualty Underwriters (CPCUs).

address:	720 Providence Road
	P.O. Box 30019
	Melvern, PA 19355
phone:	(800)932-2878

The *National Association of Real Estate Brokers* can provide information about Certified Real Estate Brokers (CRBs).

address:	430 North Michigan Avenue
	Chicago, IL 60611-4092
phone:	(312)321-4400
fax:	(312)329-8882

The *Million Dollar Round Table* can provide information about life insurance underwriters.

address:	2340 River Road
	Des Plaines, IL 60018
phone:	(312)298-1120